Praise for

I Keep Trying to Catch His Eye

"[A] beautiful and heart-wrenching work...Flashbacks to Max's childhood make him a vivid personality, and photos of him throughout render the author's grief devastatingly visceral...Maisel writes honestly...The result yields a deeply affecting testament to the fragility of life, and the human capacity for resilience."

—*Publishers Weekly*

"At the center of this beautifully written memoir by a father about his son Max, is a loving, devoted family. Ivan is a sportswriter, his clean, direct writing style is riveting and emotional. One winter day, when his son goes missing on purpose, the family unspools first in shock, then grief, and finally redemption as the author finds a letter written to him from Max from happier times. There is so much love in this memoir, the reader too, is redeemed. There is humor and grace as the Maisels find their way in the world without this beautiful soul in their midst. The family holds their memories of this original, one of a kind young man in their hearts. You will too. I couldn't put it down."

—Adriana Trigiani, bestselling author of
The Shoemaker's Wife

"This is a poignant memoir about the love that propels us to carry on and move forward after loss. Ivan Maisel gives voice to emotions that many of us have felt but few have been able to articulate."

—Adam Grant, #1 *New York Times* bestselling author of
Think Again and coauthor of *Option B*

"This is a story about grief, and loss and sorrow, yes. But it is also a story about triumph over those things, about love, devotion, and grace."

—Wright Thompson, *New York Times* bestselling author of *Pappyland*

"Having lost a child myself, it's hard for me to imagine a parent experiencing anything that is more painful. Losing a child to suicide adds another layer to the grief because we can't understand why it happened. In *I Keep Trying to Catch His Eye*, Ivan Maisel shares his family's story of losing a son to suicide. He examines some deep issues that aren't easy for us to talk about—suicide, mental health, grief, and recovery. This book will be helpful to anyone dealing with the loss of a loved one but especially to those who have been impacted by suicide."

—Tony Dungy, NBC Sports, former NFL player/head coach and member of the Pro Football Hall of Fame

"Loss and grief create a division between the uninitiated and those who speak the language. Maisel's gem of a book bravely bridges two worlds to help translate the many facets in grieving a child's death. Unvarnished and unsparing, this award-winning sportswriter turns the lens on his own journey to make sense of the unimaginable, demonstrating how we get through it without ever getting over it."

—Lee Woodruff, #1 *New York Times* bestselling author of *In an Instant*

"An intimate chronicle of abiding love." —*Kirkus*

"[A] poignant, understated memoir...Those who have lost a child will find a kindred spirit here." —*Booklist*

"For those who read this work, we see Max as he was. We see a family that makes the best they can through a time of grief. And we see that the human spirit, the will to both hold on and move on are both valid and necessary. And in that final understanding we find a way into each day's new dawn. And for that and so much more, I cannot recommend this book enough."   —Jay Paterno

"Losing a child is every parent's nightmare; losing one to suicide deepens the anguish unimaginably. Here, a father shares his grief and valuable lessons on how he carries on."   —*People Magazine*

"His deeply personal and moving book, *I Keep Trying to Catch His Eye: A Memoir of Loss, Grief, and Love,* is a testament both to a father's love and to the human soul's ability to grieve and remember and still not lose hope."   —Kerri Miller, Minnesota Public Radio

I Keep
Trying
to Catch
His Eye

I Keep Trying to Catch His Eye

A MEMOIR OF LOSS, GRIEF, AND LOVE

IVAN MAISEL

hachette
BOOKS

New York

Hachette Books
Hachette Book Group
1290 Avenue of the Americas
New York, NY 10104
HachetteGo.com
Twitter.com/HachetteBooks
Instagram.com/HachetteBooks

First Paperback Edition: September 2022

Hachette Books is a division of Hachette Book Group, Inc.

Published by Hachette Books, an imprint of Perseus Books, LLC, a subsidiary of Hachette Book Group, Inc. The Hachette Books name and logo is a trademark of the Hachette Book Group.

The publisher is not responsible for websites (or their content) that are not owned by the publisher.

Print book interior design by Amy Quinn.

Library of Congress Cataloging-in-Publication Data

Names: Maisel, Ivan, 1960- author.
Title: I keep trying to catch his eye : a memoir of loss, grief, and love / Ivan Maisel.
Description: First edition. | New York : Hachette Books, 2021.
Identifiers: LCCN 2021022739 | ISBN 9780306925740 (hardback) | ISBN 978-0-306-92576-4 (trade paperback) | ISBN 9780306925757 (ebook)
Subjects: LCSH: Parental grief. | Teenagers--Suicidal behavior.
Classification: LCC BF575.G7 M34 2021 | DDC 155.9/37085--dc23
LC record available at https://lccn.loc.gov/2021022739

ISBNs: 978-0-306-92574-0 (hardcover); 978-0-306-92576-4 (trade paperback); 978-0-306-92575-7 (ebook)

Printed in the United States of America

LSC-C

Printing 1, 2022

To Sarah
To Elizabeth
Lighthouses on my shore

Contents

I Keep
Trying
to Catch
His Eye

Chapter One

Demystifying Grief

At 7:37 on a frigid Monday night in February, the house phone rang. It was 2015—we still had a house phone. Meg had gone to a neighbor's house to play mah-jongg. Elizabeth, our high school senior, had made her ritual retreat upstairs to her room. I had opened a can of Progresso Light Zesty Santa Fe Chicken Soup. I remember that detail. I walked around the kitchen island and answered the phone.

"Is Margaret Murray there?" a male voice asked.

"This is her husband."

He identified himself as being from the sheriff's office in Monroe County, New York, which I knew to be the home of the Rochester Institute of Technology (RIT), where our middle child and only son, Max, was a junior.

"Do you know a Max Maisel?" he asked, pronouncing the last name "MAY-zul," which is how the sitcom character on Amazon pronounces it, instead of "May-ZELL," which is how my family has

1

pronounced it since arriving from eastern Europe at the turn of the twentieth century.

"He's our son. How can I help you?"

That is how you pick up the phone and find a trap door opening beneath you.

Max's car had been sitting in the parking lot at Charlotte Park for twenty-four hours. Charlotte Park sits on the shore of Lake Ontario, north of Rochester, many miles away from our home in Fairfield, Connecticut. Meg's brother Sean and his wife Deb own a vacation home a mile west of the park. Max has been coming to that home, to this park, every summer since kindergarten.

The sheriff called Meg because the car is registered in her name. He knew Max's name because Border Patrol had a record of Max driving the car into Canada. Lake Ontario is within the Border Patrol's jurisdiction because Canada is on the opposite shore.

I'm reasonably sure the sheriff asked me the last time we spoke to Max. I'm sure he asked a number of questions about Max. But I can't recount the conversation. My mind had already leaped past any logical explanation for his car being at the lake to the equally logical worst-case scenario.

Max was dead.

The sheriff told me he would call back in an hour. I took the soup off the stove, put it in a container, and shoved it into the refrigerator. I couldn't eat it. I never ate it. I stood there for five minutes, collecting my thoughts and rehearsing my phone call to Meg. I never seriously entertained thoughts of not telling her, giving her the last pain-free hour of her life, sitting in a neighbor's den shuffling marble tiles around a tabletop.

I am a master of the art of conflict avoidance. I bob and weave, nod, sidestep, smile, hope for a way out. But when the conflict is directly in my path, I try to go straight at it. Lance the boil, we say in our house. Not to mention that if I gave Meg that extra hour, she would never forgive me.

I called her.

"I need you to come home," I said, in as even a voice as I could muster.

"Is everything OK?"

I wasn't about to tell her over the phone that the light of her life was missing.

"I need you to come home," I repeated.

On a very cold night of a very cold winter, our twenty-one-year-old son Max walked off an ice-slicked pier onto the surface of Lake Ontario. We—my wife Meg, his sisters Sarah and Elizabeth, and I—presume that he walked until the ice gave way beneath him. We don't know. We will never know.

An eyewitness saw him get out of his car, an eleven-year-old SUV that once had belonged to his beloved grandfather, and walk onto the pier.

Law enforcement eventually spotted some of Max's belongings near the end of the pier, on the solid surface of the lake.

And eight weeks later, the fourth week of spring according to the calendar, Lake Ontario surrendered his body.

It would not be much of a whodunit. Those are the facts that we know. He left no note. Max wasn't much on communicating.

I Keep Trying to Catch His Eye is about the death of my son Max, the grief that engulfed our family, and how I learned to coexist with that grief.

I will not be so presumptuous as to include here how my wife and our two daughters have dealt with their grief. That consideration is pretty rich, given that what I do for a living as a journalist is become presumptuous enough to write a story and "explain" someone I hardly know. But—and this will not be the first time you read this in these pages—little is more personal than grief.

All grief is personal, and all grief is as individual as the person doing the grieving. Love is personal, too, and there is certainly no shortage of writing about love. As I wrote, I began to understand that grief, if you get past the awkward social construct that American culture has with death, is the purest expression of love for someone who is no longer here to express it back. We mourn the deepest for those whom we love the most.

We view grief warily, as an alien force that invades us when we are at our most vulnerable. I'm not going to pretend that I didn't suffer greatly when Max died. I'm not going to tell you that I didn't ache, that I no longer feel a void. But as I learned how to go on with my life, as I wrestled with and tried to make sense of my pain, I began to see the direct correlation between the love I had for the son I lost and the depth of my pain—my grief.

Grief is love.

For many years, I traveled on fall weekends with a small band of six to eight sportswriters who covered college football nationally. One of them, Chris Dufresne of the *Los Angeles Times*, married a woman I went to college with, Sheila Young. On those autumn trips, Chris brought with him an encyclopedic knowledge of the sport, a genial outlook, and a wicked sense of humor. He could be as funny in print as he was in person (the two don't always equate). We ate a lot of meals together, carpooled on the road to a lot of games.

Chris died of cancer in the spring of 2020 at the age of sixty-two, a loss that hurt all of us who knew him well. Sheila and I have remained in touch. Losing a spouse and losing a child are each uniquely awful, but Sheila and I trust each other in a way that only those who have endured such loss can. Sheila texted me a few months after Chris died to relay a sentiment she had heard from Greg Boyle, the founder of Homeboy Industries in Los Angeles: "Grief is the price we pay for love." Father Boyle is a Jesuit priest who has done remarkable work in gang intervention. He knows more about grieving that I ever will.

But there's an extra step in there. Grief is a price we pay for love. I think it's easier to consider grief as something without a cost. Grief is love. I don't think this is merely a matter of semantics. It's a viewpoint. Understanding that grief is love tempers the inevitable pain. Seeing grief as love helped me handle its all-consuming nature. Seeing grief as love made it seem less alien, less painful. We no longer had Max. We had all this love for Max, and no Max. We had his absence. That love metamorphosed into grief. There is so much about the death of a child that is more difficult to process—the generational incongruity, the unceasing what-ifs and where-would-he-bes, magical thinking that always will bedevil the four of us whom Max left behind.

I can't tell you that Max died, and a week or two later, this revelation of grief as love seared itself into my consciousness. Oh, no. I worked for that revelation. It took me many months. The story that I am about to tell you is roughly chronological. I had to learn that grief can be painful. I had to learn that in its early stages it is unrelenting. I had to learn that grief is permanent. I had to learn that accepting it helps but doesn't make it disappear. I can remember thinking, "I get it. I understand. Max was sick. I've processed why he died. I got it! I'm done! Mission accomplished. OK, where is he?"

I can't tell you how long it took me to see grief as love. I am hoping that, by describing it to you that way, it may save you some steps. Maybe it's just a mind trick, but seeing grief as love worked for me. It made grief more palatable and death, the one experience we all share, less fearsome. I am not hell-bent on turning our pain into a positive outcome. I am not driven to say that Max did not die in vain. That is a little too cloying for my palate. But if the story of my relationship with Max resonates with those who read it, then it would be nice to think that a sliver of this awfulness helped someone. If you stick with me and allow me to be the docent through my grief, maybe you won't recoil when it happens to you. Maybe you won't freeze and say or do something that makes your grieving friend feel worse, not better. Maybe you want to run away from this subject with an Olympic-qualifying time. I hear you. I felt that way before February 2015.

It is tempting, and egocentric, and slightly obnoxious, to say that if you haven't lost a child, you can't understand what it feels like. But I am delighted to say that it also happens to be true; delighted, because the death of a child is complete and overwhelming in its awfulness, and I wouldn't wish it on anyone.

Most of us willfully refuse to approach the subject of losing a child out of self-preservation. But those of you outside the ropes, those of you with the inability to understand what our kind of tragedy feels like, are the audience I have had in mind since the first anniversary of Max's death, when I began publishing what I have written. I am trying to explain this loss, illustrate it, reveal it, make it tangible enough that you won't be scared to approach it—to approach us.

I didn't start out with that mission in mind.

I am a creature of the word. I learned to read before I went to preschool. I make a living by writing. I am more facile expressing myself at the keyboard than in any other form. One of the many ways

Max and I differed is that Max found his voice looking through the eyepiece of a camera. One of the many ways life frustrated Max is that his eyeglasses served as a literal barrier between him and his camera. He tried to wear contact lenses, but he couldn't overcome the anxiety of sticking his finger in his eye. He. Could. Not. Do. It. He came home so defeated, his shoulders slumping more than usual.

Within a week of the death of our son, I began to type my thoughts into my laptop—vomit them, really. The first entry is a mash-up of thoughts, sentence fragments, about all my mind could form. It raced for days, skittering, unable to comprehend what had befallen me and the family that I am supposed to protect.

As a child, I cried easily, not the best trait for a boy in the Deep South, where ideals of manhood stood on foundations of stoicism, physical toughness, and all that other mid-twentieth-century bull-shit. Traveling through adolescence and young adulthood to full-blown, mortgage-holding, child-rearing manhood, I packed away that sensitivity, buried it really, buried it so deep in my gut that when I needed it, I had a hard time bringing it to the surface. In the weeks after Max died, I met a father in northern California who had lost a son more than two decades earlier. He told me he cries every day. He told me there is little in life as emotionally cleansing as a good cry. I understood what he said, but he may as well have been speaking French. I needed subtitles translating to me how to cry every day. What I would give now to more easily access those quick tears.

I had few examples. When my parents, Herman and Freida, grieved the deaths of their parents and siblings, I was either too young to understand it or no longer living at home. My mom and dad displayed remarkable inner strength through lives that encapsu-late the twentieth-century American Dream. They were childhood sweethearts, first-generation citizens, born and raised in Mobile, and they never left it. My dad began his career as a basketball coach at his (and my) high school, won the 1956 state title, and quit coaching at age thirty. He figured out that climbing the coaching ladder would mean leaving Mobile. Mom and Dad raised a close-knit family while each developed successful businesses. As I write, my mother is ninety-three and going strong. My sister, brother, and I always felt loved and supported. But Mom and Dad rarely trafficked in any deep emotion in public. Both of them, children of eastern European immigrants who believed in hard work and the Torah, probably in that order, came by it naturally.

And I don't mean to say that my grandparents didn't love their children. They loved them enough to make a life for them in a new country, one to which they slowly adapted as best they could. My mother grew up the sixth of seven children, and the fifth daughter. She is the first one that my grandfather allowed—and that is the correct, paternalistic verb for the 1940s—to go to college. My brother has our maternal grandfather's volume of American history, the one he studied to take his naturalization test. I haven't read it. It's in Yiddish.

My father's mother, widowed when my dad was ten, continued to run the small family grocery. Her way of expressing love: when my parents were newlyweds living paycheck to paycheck, their phone would ring. My grandmother, in her Yiddish-inflected English, would proclaim, "I baked," and hang up.

Translation: "I made food for you, my darling youngest. Come over and bring it home to your wife and family."

I remember being in the car with my dad after the fourth and final funeral of his siblings. Dad, before he finished high school, had lost his father and a sister. But he had the good fortune to make it well into his sixties before he lost his brother and his other two sisters.

Dad was driving home from the funeral, I was alongside in the front seat, and about five minutes removed from the cemetery, he burst into tears. He wiped his face with one hand, kept the other on the wheel, and had stopped crying before we hit the next red light.

And yet my dad was a warm, funny parent who communicated love through humor and deed. In the business world he drove himself and his employees hard and drove his deals harder. When he had to confront the big, painful emotions, in himself and others, he believed in the shortest path.

I walked into the house one afternoon during my sophomore year of high school. I turned into the den and found my dad home from work, a rare occurrence in midafternoon. He was sitting in a chair, and in the picture I have in my head, my mother stood next to him.

"Ivan," he said. "Your dog is dead."

That story eventually became the source of great hilarity among me, my sister, and my brother. We usually added a response from me, something like, "Fine, and you?"

My point is that when it came to the big, painful emotions, my parents held them at bay. Mom and Dad didn't dwell, at least within the scope of my eyesight. My mother's favorite saying, for as long as I can recall, has been, "This too shall pass." That is what I knew. When my dad died at age eighty-one in 2007, seven and a half years before Max died, I couldn't have been more poorly equipped to handle it. So I didn't—avoidance masked as optimism, avoidance masked as consideration—as he descended into hospice care, as he donned the armor of morphine to ease his final days. I didn't race back to my hometown. When I did return home, I didn't race to his bedside. Instead of acknowledging that I didn't want to confront his death, I told myself all kinds of stories.

He won't know I'm there.

I didn't want to bother him.

And the best one: I didn't want to bring up that he was dying. As I look back, I'm pretty sure he knew.

I so wrapped myself in avoidance that providing comfort to my dad never became my primary consideration. Only recently, having gained the wisdom of grief, have I come to understand that I had a model for how to handle my father's demise all along: my father.

My uncle Max, my son's namesake, had health issues throughout his life. He spent nearly a decade of his childhood in a hospital, battling a bone infection in the days before sulfa drugs. My father, three years younger, devoted himself to his brother from an early age. Dad worked as a teenaged soda jerk in Joe Bear's drugstore, not far from the old Mobile Infirmary. Every day, when Mr. Bear wasn't looking, my dad would pour the cream off the top of the milk bottle, make Uncle Max a thick-as-mud milkshake and take it over to the infirmary on his bike.

More than a half century later, as Uncle Max succumbed to cancer at age sixty-eight, he allowed virtually no visitors into his house except for his brother. Dad went over there every day, made lunch for the two of them, and comforted Uncle Max. They talked, they didn't talk, they sat, they communed. *Comforted.*

If I had to make a bracket of behavior in my life that I would like to have back, my father's last weeks would make at least the semifinals. I lived in denial. I didn't prepare our kids very well. They last saw their Papaw two months before he died, at my niece's wedding. Dad made sure he stuck around for that. Rather than prepare Sarah, Max, and Elizabeth to say goodbye, I lived in a world where I thought, "Look at him. He's hanging in there. We'll see him at Thanksgiving." Dad made it to his sixtieth wedding anniversary in September. He barely reached October.

I cheated my kids out of a valuable life lesson. But I hadn't learned the lesson, either. If Google Maps laid out my route to emotional maturity, the message on my route would read, "30 yrs longer." That was the person I was when Max died. I didn't know how to grieve.

In those first days and weeks after Max disappeared, I understood intuitively that I had to do something to proactively excavate the layers and layers of pain from my innards. If I couldn't cry, if I couldn't emote in public, I could open my laptop and type. So I did, most mornings, sometimes before sunrise, for months. It became second nature to me. Giving my thoughts a voice, bringing them into the light, crystallized them, made them and the emotions they described feel more substantive.

Dealing with death demands emotional maturity from everyone in its path, from the survivors, to friends called upon to support them, to acquaintances just learning the news. The demands are different, depending on the griever's relationship to the deceased, but no less incessant. You choose either to accede or push it away.

I gradually came to understand that I had to grieve, express my pain, give voice to my loss. I also understood that my friends, my acquaintances, my work contacts were not compelled to listen. Plenty of them did. We benefited from so many kindnesses, small and large. But plenty did not. Their lives did not compel them to confront this pain. So why confront it? Why acknowledge it? Why connect to discomfort?

A woman in our neighborhood described to Meg how she couldn't attend the memorial service we had for Max because it would have been too emotionally difficult for her.

"It's nice that you had a choice," Meg replied. I'm not sure if the woman ever noticed the shiv in her ribs.

I have been on the receiving end of a litany of well-meaning, perfunctory responses: reassurances that Max has gone to a better place; queries whether after weeks or months I felt better (as if my losing Max could be cured with an antibiotic); the question, "Is it still hard?"; or no response at all.

I do not like euphemisms, unless they are employed for humor. I do not like "passed away." I do not like "no longer with us," "gone to his glory," or "met his Maker." Max died. He is dead, and softening the language doesn't soften the blow. Sugarcoating doesn't make it easy for anyone but the person saying it, the person who may tiptoe around the loss with cloaked language and continue on with his day.

The survivors aren't the ones who need the euphemism. We confront the death of our loved ones every day. We must learn to coexist with loss. Softening the language doesn't change that task. You might be able to convince me that "passed away" is a well-meaning courtesy. My personal experience is that, in the throes of loss, when the sinkhole inside me felt as if it would expand until it consumed every ounce of mind and body, "He's gone to a better place" soothed nothing.

I did take solace that Max's death meant an end to his suffering. But I don't like to think that Max has joined my father, my brother-in-law Mike, and my sister-in-law Annie in the Great Beyond. Well, I like to think it. I just don't want to put a lot of stock in that thought being anything more than a calming wish. In most cases, when I refer to Max's death, I say "death," not "passing."

I saw my former self in that softened language. I saw my former self among those who spoke to me and pretended that his death didn't happen, or the people who said something once and considered that box checked. Because that had been me, I was charitable when my emotional doppelgängers approached me. I could size them up in an instant and see how I had evolved. I could see the path I had hacked out of my emotional underbrush.

I began, slowly, to try to explain publicly how this loss felt. I believed then, and believe now, that if I described what grief felt like, maybe it would be demystified. Maybe those who heard me, or those who read me, wouldn't be so scared of death.

As I wrote about my grief, as I wrote of other parents who became members of the Club No One Wants to Join, the responses from those not in the club encouraged me to continue forward. They also underlined the differences in our lives. Regularly, I was told how "courageous" I was. They would focus not on the message but on the "courage" it took to write the message.

After I did a video piece for ESPN *College GameDay* and wrote a story about Mark and Kym Hilinski, whose son Tyler, a Washington State quarterback, ended his life in January 2018, the Henry W. Grady College of Journalism at the University of Georgia asked me to speak that fall at its annual McGill Symposium for Journalistic Courage.

I have to say, I didn't get it.

The notion of courage implies a choice, that the four of us chose to undertake this more difficult course as if we got off a chairlift and looked for the steepest, bumpiest descent. Max became ill, and Max died. It hit us hard. The added burden of suicide, and of societal views toward mental illness, made processing his death more difficult. We came to believe that it's every bit as deadly as cancer and more insidious, and there is no x-ray or MRI that will reveal it.

All of it—the death, the mental illness, the many questions, the few, unsatisfying answers—devastated our lives. One phone call from law enforcement in Rochester stripped me and Meg of the foolish belief that we led a charmed life, that we would continue to live as we had lived for fifty-five years, largely devoid of heartbreak, free of pain.

If we made a choice, it was to continue to exist, to live our lives, to breathe. There were days when that took courage. In the weeks after Max died, I once drove two towns away to shop for groceries, a different place where I pretended for forty-five minutes that my life had returned to normal. I wandered up and down the aisles, secure in the knowledge that I would see no one from the life where my son had died, that I would not have to deal with questions from friends, that I would not be on the receiving end of stares as the father of that boy who had been on the front page of the newspaper for days. I could chitchat with the woman at the register. It felt like Disney-land. It felt as if I had escaped to my old life. It was an artificial high, illicit and intoxicating, with returns that would diminish rapidly if I kept trying to achieve it.

That was one great, uncourageous trip to the grocery store. When I checked out, I loaded the groceries into my car, locked it, and walked back to the wine shop next to the grocery store. I walked up and down those aisles, too.

But after I drove home, what courage that existed came simply in the decision to continue to get out of bed, to undertake the enormous task of accepting that we had to go on without Max. It took no courage at all to write about my grief. Writing is what I do. It is how I communicate.

As it became clear to me that my view of our lives differed from what our friends and acquaintances saw, my desire to write on this topic began to grow. I want to tell you about Max, about me and Max, about me and no Max, which is about me and my grief. What follows in these pages is largely my experience. Trust me, there are some very sad moments. There are also uplifting moments, and funny, and embarrassing, and entertaining moments, and everything else that happens to human beings. Grievers continue to live their lives.

Ten weeks after Max died, two weeks after his body surfaced in Lake Ontario, our nephew got married in my hometown of Mobile. I believed that the four of us should attend the wedding. To say we attended with mixed emotions is the understatement of the century. Meg probably would tell you her emotions weren't mixed at all. She didn't want to go. Only with the perspective of hindsight do I understand the enormity of her sacrifice. But we came to the realization that if we did not attend, then we would be projecting our pain more deeply into our extended family. We didn't want Max's death to be the horrible gift that keeps on giving. I had visions of our absence hanging over the wedding, that weekend and for years to come.

The wedding made clear, even though it happened well before the four of us could embrace the message, that as we adjusted to the searing pain of losing Max, good things would continue to happen in our lives.

We endured the wedding more than we enjoyed it. But we ate and we drank and we danced, and we did celebrate. Fake it until you make it. For fifty-five years, I had dodged the truly, epically awful. Meg and I are part of the demographic cohort that evaded one American scourge after another. We're white, straight, grew up middle- to upper-middle class. Old enough to miss the polio scare, young enough to miss serving in Vietnam, old enough not to worry about AIDS in college, young enough to miss thinking that cigarettes personified cool. To me, it was all part of the charmed-life package.

And then our boy went missing.

Chapter Two

Hey, Bud!

At first, Max smiled for the camera.
Photo courtesy of the Maisel Family

Our second child came into this world on January 15, 1994, with both of us crying: him, as an eight-pound, three-ounce baby, me as the father who got to tell his father that the family had a new Max Maisel. My father's only brother, Max, doted on me until the day he died, three years earlier. I was so excited that we had a boy, that we again had a Max Maisel in our family, that as I attempted to take photos of him on the baby scale, I fumbled the camera, which hit the tile floor of the delivery room and never worked again.

In public, Max didn't enter a room as much as he slid quietly along the wall. I should tell you that at home, he never entered the room quietly. When Max came down our stairs, he hit each step in a way that sounded somewhere between a gallop and a rockslide.

Max always marched to his own beat. As a toddler, he didn't like loud noises, new foods, or itchy tags. He was on his own planet and happy to be there. He had the same cute verbal tics that most toddlers have. For instance, when prompted to express gratitude, his entire face would break into a smile and he would say, "Thank you you're welcome!" After some time, however, we began to realize that some quirks are different than others. Actually, we didn't realize it. It never occurred to us that Max's ability at age three to recite the entire text of *The Sneetches* (a Dr. Seuss classic) could be interpreted as anything other than cute. But a neighborhood mom recognized it as echolalia, a pathological condition. Our neighbor and close friend Brian Barlaam, a school psychologist, saw other characteristics as potential issues as well. We intervened with every available resource—special preschool, speech therapy, occupational therapy, physical therapy, psychologists, specialists—we spent the GNP of several small countries having him tested for a number of years, all to find out he resided "somewhere on the learning disorder spectrum."

What do you do with that? Inexact science may sound like an oxymoron, but there is no x-ray that can diagnose autism, no shadow on an MRI that announces itself as Asperger's. Max never received a diagnosis of either. I don't believe "none of the above" is the name of a learning disorder, but that is what Max had to overcome. We as parents and Max himself just did the best we could. Max needed one-on-one attention, and we had the good fortune to have the resources to provide it. As a middle schooler, Max began seeing a therapist, a man who became one of the few people Max allowed inside his walls. I believe in therapy. If talking to someone can make you feel better, why wouldn't you give it a try? I went through a period of depression in my early forties. The boy who learned to tamp down his emotions—me—may have learned a little too well. I struggled with my work and brought those struggles into the rest of my life. My therapist, Debra Belanger, has been a special person in my life for nearly two decades. I still go see her, now more as a 7,500-mile checkup. My point is that Max going to therapy didn't make me blink at all. Once he went to college, he began taking an antidepressant, Prozac. I don't know what it did for him, but Max taking it made me feel better. A similar drug helped pull my wagon out of the ditch fifteen years before.

The point is that a lot went on between Max's ears, most of which he guarded carefully. As I said, he let very few—actually, close to none—inside his gates. He did this for self-preservation. It was a learned behavior. As a small boy, he had trouble grasping social cues. As he got older, he understood them, but they remained a second language. With his differences, he gained an early understanding of who he was. He would not do anything because everyone else did it. To put it another way, he would not do anything *because* everyone else did it. Sometimes I think it was plain old stubbornness. But to me it seemed that it always came from a place of self-preservation.

We live in a small neighborhood in which a lot of families had children roughly the same age. Max had ten kids in a three-street area with whom he attended school from kindergarten through twelfth grade. Max lived down the street, and on a different planet. He had no interest in the rough-and-tumble of backyard play, whether it was sports or not. As far as we could determine, the other neighborhood kids accepted Max. They let him be, which was both good and bad.

On the one hand, they didn't pick on him. On the other, my memories of Max are of him alone. Alone in a swimming pool of children, alone in a crowd, alone with a book, alone with his Pokémon cards, alone on a weekend night. Even I, the less extroverted of his parents, thought Max needed more social interaction. It just didn't come naturally to him. By second grade, his teacher noted that Max "has trouble compromising, inviting other children to play, and giving compliments.... Max [is] a child who is easily embarrassed, has temper tantrums and often appears lonely and sad."

Our friend Ellen Reilly told us a story of Max at a young age, wandering around the neighborhood Memorial Day party by himself. You have to understand: this party felt like it included pretty much everyone in the zip code. Max wandered around, alone per usual, and Ellen called him over to where she was sitting with her daughter Charlotte, Max's classmate. Ellen asked him about the party, and if he was having a good time, and he answered, and she tried to chat him up, and he never knew how to do that, so the conversation came to a close. Max wandered off, but Ellen remembered he quickly, quietly came back to where she and Charlotte were sitting and sat down a few feet away. As much as he shrunk from conversation as the grease of human interaction, he wanted the connection. He wanted the connection.

I am no psychologist, but it always seemed to me that Max's social difficulties had some tie to his resistance to change, as if he needed to know he could depend on the items he allowed into his existence. For instance, no pickier eater ever ate a French fry. As a young boy, his food rarely strayed from various shades of brown. He drank more milk and ate more Double Stufs than any four people you've ever met. Proust had his madeleines. Max had his Oreos. After Max died, I often got emotional walking down the cookie aisle of the grocery (the truth is, my stomach still flips). I would assess every Double Stuf product tweak—Convenience Pack! Family Size! King Size! Mega Stuf!—according to what I knew of Max's standards. Same with the cereal aisle. Every time I see a new flavor of Cap'n Crunch, I go to Max for a few seconds.

For the record, I believe he would have said yes to Cap'n Crunch Airheads and no to Cap'n Crunch Cotton Candy Crunch. I would describe Max as a classicist.

That is to say, Max's limited tolerance for change found its home in his menu. Getting older brought on changes and challenges that, given the choice, he never would have confronted. But we left him alone on food, and he stayed within his well-stocked comfort zone. Max subsisted on protein and carbs: sugared cereals, Double Stuf Oreos, Utz pretzel rods, Martinelli's apple juice, red meat, chicken, French fries, Honeycrisp apples. On his eighteenth birthday, Max got eighteen different brands of cereals. If memory serves, Kellogg's All-Bran was not among them. Milk. Max liked nothing carbonated—no Cokes, no root beers, no seltzers. He drank *a lot* of milk.

Sandwiches failed whatever test he gave them. Hamburger buns did as well. He liked his hamburgers and steaks medium-well, grayer than a New England winter. Max had a spiel he would go through with each waitperson. He learned through repetition to be precise in his instructions. No bun, just the meat, well done, no garnish. If "no garnish" got a quizzical look, he elaborated. No lettuce, no tomato, no onion, no nothing. By the time he said, "And fries," the waitperson had figured out to pay close attention, write everything down, and repeat.

Our favorite hot dog joint in Fairfield is called Super Duper Weenie. Gary, the proprietor, a classically trained chef, began selling hot dogs and sausages out of a food truck. We hired the truck for a couple of house parties, so we had become, if not regulars, at least known. Several years after Super Duper Weenie opened, Gary added grass-fed six-ounce burgers to his menu. Max would order them medium-well. Carmina, who ran the counter, would take the order and call it out to Gary, his back to the register. He didn't even look up to see who would do that to his beautiful beef.

"You're killing me, Max!" Gary would shout. "Killing me!"

My standard definition of my actual relationship with my son is that Max's nearly complete lack of interest in sports proved that God had a sense of humor. It turns out that mothers have genes, too. In physical terms, Max couldn't, wouldn't, didn't put on weight. Meg found among Max's social media effects a couple of OkCupid questionnaires he filled out just days before he died. One of the lines that stood out to me—made me smile, really: "I have a love/hate relationship with my comical tallness."

He stood six foot five, in and of itself not funny. The comedy came in his frame. Max weighed 135 pounds, if his pockets were full. Physically, he was pure Murray, built like his maternal grandfather and uncles—a big, thick mop of hair, eyelashes that women pay big money to approximate, and less than no ass. I mean none. His pants needed a court order to keep from sliding below his hips. He pretty much refused to wear a belt. He lived in sweats and tracksuit pants. The problem is that the elastic waistbands had to perform all the work on their own. Nothing in Max's midsection expanded to greet the elastic. Meg resorted to buying two pairs of khakis and taking them to a tailor, who would cannibalize one pair to lengthen the legs on the other.

Max also had an aversion to buttons, stemming from trouble with them when he was little. He wore dress shirts only on demand. He existed in T-shirts covered, if weather demanded, by (unbuttoned) thick flannel shirts or hoodies.

Nor did Max have an athletic bone in his body. Well, that's not entirely true. He began skiing at age seven and over time developed into a graceful skier, competent on any terrain. He did love the pool, even if he only tolerated swimming. Give him a pair of goggles, a snorkel, and a penny, and he could entertain himself for a couple of hours.

Nevertheless, we signed him up for T-ball. We have a baseball card of him in uniform, glove on his left hand, big smile on his face. But Max didn't love it. He didn't even like it. I helped coach the first season. I told myself it was for his peace of mind. Clearly it was for mine. I wanted to be there in case his behavior needed a translation to the other dads who coached. If he hit one ball out of the infield, he didn't hit another one. He made it through the first season, and we automatically signed him up for the next one. Bad move. At the first practice, I remember him being in the outfield, caterwauling about something. I walked out there, put my arm around him, and we walked off the field together, Max explaining to me at the top of his lungs, "I hate baseball! I don't want to play!"

We didn't go back.

He was solitary enough that I thought he might find an outlet in golf, a game that has enchanted and tormented me for much of my life. Max declined a second trip to the practice range. I wish I had asked again.

What I never completely understood, though, is that he never became a sports fan. In my pre-parental naivete, I believed that if I had a son, he would grow up with the same insatiable hunger for sports that I had as a child. My son would learn math through baseball statistics. He would collect baseball and football cards. He would entertain himself for summer hours on end playing baseball board games, baseball dice games, baseball games with a rubber ball in the garage—again, sorry about that window, Mom—and an eighteen-hole plastic-ball golf course in the yard.

Again, sorry about the divots, Mom.

Max would watch the games I covered, and the minute I walked in the door on Sunday, he would pepper me with questions until I begged him to stop. But that wasn't our Max. When he agreed to go to sporting events, he enjoyed them, drinking in the spectacle and eating his favorite treats—if you think about it, Max's menu dovetailed nicely with a ballpark menu.

I have a photo of him, seven years old, sitting in a box seat at Shea Stadium, dwarfed by the immensity of his surroundings. We saw Barry Bonds hit number fifty-six of his seventy-three home runs that summer—August 27, 2001, two weeks and a day before the horrors of 9/11.

Max at Shea Stadium, 2001
Photo courtesy of the Maisel Family

Max and I with his NBA Lego set. This is as close as he came to being a sports fan.
Photo courtesy of the Maisel Family

When Max was nine years old, Lego produced an NBA set. The only way I knew this is that out of the blue, Max asked me about Kevin Garnett and Kobe Bryant. Actually, he asked me about Kevin GAR-nit and KOHB Bryant. He rendered me speechless, nonetheless. He had been reading a Lego catalog. Well before the 24-second clock expired, we were in the car, headed to Toys "R" Us. The New Jersey Nets, an hour and a half from our house, were represented in the set by Jason Kidd. When the next NBA season rolled around, I asked Max if he wanted to see Kidd play in person.

I thought I had established a beachhead. Max had watched me read the sports page at breakfast every morning that we have ever eaten breakfast together. During the NBA Playoffs, when I asked Max if he wanted to read the game story of the Nets' victory, he said yes.

Max read the copy on the front of the sports section, D1. He looked up and asked, "Where is page D3?"

We attended several games a year for three or four years. The trips, usually ninety minutes each way, turned out to be the most regular one-on-one time I ever created with him. We had other moments, and we took a few trips together, but the Nets games became a ritual. Max, remember, liked the tried and true. For instance, he would get the same food at every game: chicken tenders, French fries, and an enormous cup of bright red Hawaiian Punch pregame, soft ice cream at halftime.

As the cheerleaders led the team onto the court, including four men holding big flagpoles, I would make the same dad joke every game. We sat opposite the high-rolling fans, so we saw the flags backwards.

"Max," I would say, "what is S-T-E-N?"

By the third year, I would start in a fake announcer voice, "You know, Max, I can't help but wonder . . . " Before I could ask the question, he would put up his hand. "Stop, or I will hurt you," he would say. I loved that he played along with the joke.

Max didn't know a pick-and-roll from a cinnamon roll, but he became fascinated by the pressure of the 24-second clock, and he loved to watch the stats to see whether anyone neared a triple-double (double figures in three of four categories: points, rebounds, assists, steals).

In the end, I knew that Max could live without fandom. Our house became the venue for the neighborhood Super Bowl party. Max never emerged from the basement to watch the game. And that was pro football. Max grew up in a family that focused on college football. For one thing, his groceries depended on it—I have covered college football nationally since 1987. For another, the paternal side of his family, save for the stray cousin or in-law, are devoted Alabama football fans. I grew up in the home of two Alabama graduates and was indoctrinated accordingly (for professional reasons, such as credibility, I have learned to put that affinity in my back pocket while working). Thanksgiving is the most important annual event on the Maisel calendar. My father was born on Thanksgiving Day 1925; the college football nerd in me is delighted to tell you that on that day, his future alma mater, the University of Alabama, clinched its first Rose Bowl bid by defeating Georgia, 27–0. I could go on, but the editor would delete it. Rightfully so.

Because we celebrated Dad's birthday, the holiday took on a festive air that extended beyond turkeys and pilgrims. We have had as many as forty-five people attend our Thanksgiving meals in Mobile, and we're related to most of them. Thanksgiving weekend during Max's life often included the Iron Bowl, Alabama's annual football rivalry with intrastate rival Auburn, either on television or in person. When Max tagged along to Tuscaloosa, he did so to hang out with his cousins, not because the tenor of his next 365 days depended on the outcome of the game.

Max, a black-and-white person in a gray world, had been trained by three generations to feel a certain way about Auburn. I travel there regularly, and I have developed friendships over thirty-five years of covering college football. That was a subtlety that escaped our twelve-year-old son. I once introduced the sports information director to Max as "my friend from Auburn, Kirk Sampson," to which Max reflexively replied, "But, Dad—you hate Auburn!"

Maybe that's how Max learned to hold grudges, granting a merciful pardon only when he had no choice, as with me and Meg, or with his beloved ski instructor in Steamboat Springs, Colorado, Josh Berkowitz. Josh pushed Max past his fears and made him into a skier comfortable anywhere on the mountain. But Josh made the high-school-age Max so mad one year that Max just stopped talking to him. When we learned of this, we told Max that was fine. He could just ski with his mother and father all day.

Max found it in his heart to forgive Josh.

Having said all of that, I must tell you that I never swallowed my disappointment in Max. I was never disappointed.

Max may have had little interest in sports, but he found things that he could make his own and he adopted them: You could draw a direct line in Max's interests, from Thomas the Tank Engine to dinosaurs to Bionicles to Legos to Pokémon to Beyblades to Harry Potter to anime to manga to the TV show *Survivor* to the movies of Christopher Nolan. He had no use for popular music, but he liked video-game soundtracks. He maintained an unabashed enthusiasm for Broadway musicals and comedy. I have a distinct memory of his cantilevered frame doubled over in laughter watching James Corden's physical brand of ass-over-teakettle humor in *One Man, Two Guvnors*. I had constructed a bridge to Max out of slapstick and wordplay years before.

For instance, I introduced our children at a young age to *Duck Soup*, the Marx brothers' farce. For the next, oh, two years after Max's initial viewing, he would walk up to me and restage one of Groucho's signature bits. Max would call me swine, I would call him upstart, and he would pretend to slap me. Max loved Bugs and Daffy, and he loved the radio comedy of Bob and Ray. Both duos delighted in timing and wordplay. They delivered a lot of punch lines that remained in use in our house for years. (I would give you an example, but anytime anyone in our house delivered a punch line, failed to get the desired laugh, and then attempted to steer the audience to the laugh, Max would thunder, "Don't explain the joke!")

"I smile when I think about Max uttering a dry but witty remark under his breath, just loud enough so that classmates right in his vicinity could hear his remark," Julia Fedoryk, Max's high school Latin teacher, told Genevieve Reilly, who wrote a nice, sensitive piece in the *Fairfield Citizen* about Max after he disappeared. "Max deserved the respect he got from peers because he earned it. I remember seeing them turn quickly in surprise and admiration for his quick wit and subtle delivery. I remember hearing that sense of humor come out at the most charming moments."

As a teenager, Max devoted himself to *Survivor* and to *Whose Line Is It Anyway?*, the long-running improv show. As his sensibilities began to mature, Max drifted to the commentary of Jon Stewart, Stephen Colbert, and John Oliver. Because Max's resting face rarely strayed from deadpan—part of his self-protection mechanism—I continued to employ him as a straight man for my dad jokes. When Elizabeth had her wisdom teeth removed three weeks after Max disappeared, I was annoyed that he wasn't around to hear me ask her a question I asked him all the time:

"Max, does your face hurt?"

As he got older, he began replying, "No, but yours is killing me, and I don't know why you even bother."

Some time after Max died, Meg reminded me how much she cherished that when I walked into the house and saw him, my whole countenance lightened. I broke into a smile, and I said, "Hey, Bud!" Some of my attitude was stagecraft. Max didn't possess the tools to connect with people. As his natural reticence and insecurities blended with adolescent angst, I made sure that my delight in seeing him would be out front for him and everyone else to see. Mostly him.

Max, age ten, flanked by his grandfathers, John Murray (*left*) and Herman Maisel
Photo courtesy of Clare Murray Volo

I stole "Bud" from my dad, who always called Max "my best buddy." My father's love for Max was unconditional. His love for all ten of his grandchildren was unconditional. He smothered them in attention and wet, slobbery "tante" kisses to their cheeks, exaggerated from the kisses his aunts (tantes) gave him in his childhood. But he took a special interest in Max. Part of that, surely, was that Max was named for his beloved brother. On the day Max was born, Dad wrote him a letter of "welcome into the world of the Maisels."

"My heart is full and I thank God for giving you to me as a source of comfort in the autumn of my life," my sixty-eight-year-old dad wrote.

But there was more to Dad's love than Max's name. He didn't know everything about Max's issues. But he seemed to understand at some primal level that Max needed his love and support, and Dad provided it without hesitation or question. Max responded to it. When Meg and I would bring the kids to Mobile, inevitably my dad would pull Meg aside and rave to her about how well Max was doing, how he had matured since his last visit. After Max died, Mom told me that any time she had expressed concern about Max, Dad would say, "Don't worry about him. He's gonna be all right." Dad may have seen Max through a grandfather's rose-colored glasses. I took it as unconditional, unquestioning love.

Max's maternal grandfather, John Murray, felt the same way about him. When Max visited his Oma (Nancy) and Opa in upstate New York, he and John made countless trips together to the Syracuse Zoo and to the Museum of Science and Technology.

One of my favorite pictures of Max is of him standing with John in our driveway. Max loved being behind the camera and hated being in front of it. But he also understood family dynamics and the importance of multigenerational photos, and he loved his Opa. Max looks to be fifteen or sixteen, already taller than his tall grandfather, and his shoulders are back and his head high. He is actually posing. We have very few of those.

John took Max's death as hard as anyone outside the four of us.

It is not easy, as a helicopter parent of long standing, to say that Max lived a difficult life. But all the evidence points to the conclusion that our hovering turned out to be no match for the challenges he tried to surmount for twenty-one years.

From an early age, Max saw the world as half empty. In one sense, he had reason to. Max had the most physical difficulties of our three children. He never slept well. Ever. He had trouble gripping a pencil, which led to handwriting that started out hard to decipher and never improved. He had the most ear infections. He endured regular allergy shots for several years. Is there anything more terrifying for a child than the dread of regular shots? We eventually came up with a routine: I taught him Lamaze breathing, the nurse would count down before injecting him, and after the shot, we would go for a post-hypodermic milkshake.

That structure helped him cope with the anticipatory fear of the pain. Max loved structure. As the child of two rule followers, he got every rule-following gene his parents possess, to the point of rigidity. Normal teenagers see the world in black and white. They are too young, perhaps too idealistic, to discern the grays where people actually live. Max didn't live among the norms. His blacks and whites rarely mixed. You either followed the rules or you didn't: parental rules, societal rules, rules Max created for the people around him. Max did well when told what to do.

"Max, can you walk Cece?"

"On it, bossman. C'mon, you stupid mutt." ("Stupid mutt," by the way, served as teenaged Max's form of affection.)

The rule following may be due to birth order, or it may just have been his personality. One of Meg's fondest memories of his last days at home is of Max walking into the kitchen, opening the dishwasher, and beginning to unload it.

"Max?" she asked.

"I knew you were going to ask me to do it, anyway," he said.

Again, no psychologist here, just a parent who loved his son and didn't always know how to reach him. But it seems to me that Max clung to the rigidity of his rules as someone would hold on to a light pole in a windstorm. Most of us learn to negotiate our way through the swirl of daily life. To Max, that swirl felt more like a maelstrom too dangerous to enter. He stayed where he felt comfortable, anchored to the familiar. Following the rules kept him tethered to normalcy in a world he had so much difficulty deciphering. He feared getting into trouble. He feared a lot of things. If something proved difficult, he got anxious, overwhelmed. Rather than work harder, he tended to shut down.

At the end of second grade, Max took a battery of speech and language tests. The clinician noted that after a while, Max began to get frustrated. He had become sophisticated about the testing game. "Several times the clinician needed to stop and talk to Max about how he was feeling," the report stated, "at which time he would ask how many more wrong he needed to get so that the test would end."

I'm sorry. That still makes me laugh.

His teachers began to figure out that they needed to go over with him all the possible outcomes of a new situation. Still, as he moved into preadolescence, he began to deal with stress by plucking his long, beautiful eyelashes. That habit lasted a couple of years.

In fifth grade, Max lied to us about something; I don't remember what. When we busted him, I told him his punishment would be to write a report on President Nixon's Watergate cover-up. Those seeds bore much sweeter fruit than I imagined. Several years later, the movie *Frost/Nixon* riveted Max. He watched it more than once. As he grew older, his natural introversion began to morph into a dry, sardonic take on everyone and everything around him. As he reached adolescence, his dark side appeared darker. He wrote a three-stanza poem in seventh grade that repeated four times the line, "I am an isolator from everyone and a silent speaker." This was the final stanza:

> *I understand that I may never be truly happy.*
> *I say that sometimes the only way to win is to*
> *   clear the board completely.*
> *I dream that I will be free from my nightmares.*
> *I try to be a peacemaker between friends.*
> *I hope that I will eventually become truly happy.*
> *I am an isolator from everyone and a silent speaker.*

It is easy, now that we know the end to his sad movie, to say that a child writing something like that in middle school should have set off alarm bells. Meg confronted his teacher and his guidance counselor to ask why we hadn't been notified. Then she asked Max why he wrote it.

"'Clear the board,'" Max repeated, drawing it out for emphasis. "Ever hear of a metaphor, Mom?"

His humor tempered my reaction to the poem. What he wrote didn't upset me as much as the realization that, even at that age, Max had established a pattern of being alone. It wasn't by choice. In elementary school, and again in middle school, Max would make a friend, be utterly devoted to that friend, and when that boy would move along, Max would be devastated. He didn't have it in him to do what the other child had done—make another friend. Such behavior didn't come easily to him. As he got older, as hormones began to intervene, as he reached adolescence, when kids become more cliquey, when they become more interested in sex, it became even more difficult for him. He had so little confidence in himself, and so little belief that anything good would happen to him, that when he did suffer a setback, he reacted as if he had expected it to happen.

Like many American kids, Max became obsessed with Pokémon, the Japanese anime card game. I write that descriptive phrase fully understanding that for Max's generation, that is the redundancy of the clueless, as if in my teen years someone had written "baseball, the Americanized version of rounders that came to be the national pastime." As a father who still owns the baseball cards he collected in the 1960s and 1970s, I could relate, even if the rules of Pokémon sounded as dissonant to me as baseball stats did to Max. On those occasions when we played the card game, he stacked the deck to make sure he would win. But even on a straight deal, I never really understood the rules. Max didn't depend on me to play. He discovered a Saturday morning gathering a couple of towns away where Pokémon enthusiasts brought their decks to battle one another. He enjoyed going, but he made little effort to befriend the other players.

Meg and I convinced him he should approach a local hobby store to create that same kind of gathering closer to home. The store owners, a lovely couple in our local Jewish community, agreed to give him some space. They put up a sign in the window. Max was willing to try to get some friends at school to join him. What he did, how loudly he beat the drum, I don't know. I know one friend agreed to go. With great fanfare from us, Max went to the store ready to play.

When we picked him up ninety minutes later, no one had come. He was crestfallen, and he felt betrayed. We told him not to be discouraged, that it would take time for word of mouth to build, that he should keep trying.

Max went back to the store one or two more afternoons at the scheduled times, and no one ever came. This attempt produced no connections with his peers, and he retreated into his shell. As I recount this episode, I know it may sound as if all Max had to do was go back to school and cajole his friends to join him. In retrospect, I may as well have been encouraging him to sit down at the piano and play a Bach concerto. He was equipped to do neither, and even as I began to understand how difficult the day-to-day was for him, I never committed myself to figuring out how to help him.

Perhaps we shouldn't have been proactive; we shouldn't have put him in a position to fail. (Of course, I also beat myself up for not being more proactive as the parent of a child who ended his life, but I'll get to that.) Throughout his teens, I continued to believe that Max would outgrow his doom and gloom, outmaneuver it, just learn to live with it. I still don't know how much was wishful thinking, and how much a blind eye toward what would become a fatal mental illness. I'm not sure I want to see that final scorecard.

Chapter Three

College

I don't allow myself to indulge in too many sliding-door moments with Max. A sliding-door moment—maybe you saw the Gwyneth Paltrow film *Sliding Doors*—is an either/or decision that alters everything that follows. There are few doors more important than the one a high school senior chooses to slide open for college. Whether Max would have survived his illness had he attended another university . . . I used the verb "indulge" for a reason. That sort of thinking is a luxury. Dreaming of Max at Tulane or the University of New Hampshire or Binghamton or Fairfield University, seven minutes from our house, amounted to little more than a waste of time.

Sometimes you slide open a door just to go anywhere else but where you are.

Max didn't cast as wide a geographic net in his college search as his older sister Sarah had. He did what most kids do—he looked within driving radius of family. That included Tulane, two hours from Mobile, where he had three generations of family. Tulane kids work hard and they play hard—it is New Orleans. But in the end, universities with reputations as party schools held no allure for him. Max chose to attend RIT, located in a city that he had visited nearly every summer of his life. Meg and I wondered aloud whether perhaps a gap year would be appropriate. Max didn't act as emotionally mature as his age. But he told Meg that if he didn't go to college right after high school, he wouldn't go at all, and we let the idea of a gap year expire.

RIT had a curriculum uniquely suited for Max. As is true with many introverts, Max found the best way to communicate his thoughts and feelings was from behind the camera. Max could express himself through photography with more facility than through writing or speaking, although even with a camera in hand he avoided people. He preferred to photograph architecture, nature, the juxtaposition of objects to one another. Max discovered his affinity for photography at a young age. One day on vacation in Steamboat Springs, we wandered into the studio of Don Tudor, whose breathtaking work captures the flora and fauna of Colorado. Don is a warm, gentle soul; we became enthralled with his prints. Two hang in our home. Max saw them every day.

When Max graduated high school, I told him to pick out a place for a celebratory trip. Most kids wanted the beach. Max and I went to Chicago for three days, which he spent photographing buildings and public art he had researched. I stood behind him with my iPhone poised.

Every time he took a picture, I took a picture of him taking a picture: at Buckingham Fountain in Grant Park, the *Cloud Gate* sculpture in Millennium Park, the juxtaposition of the modern One Illinois Center and the Beaux Arts look of the Wrigley Building, the

Taking photos of architecture in Chicago after high school graduation in 2012
Photo courtesy of the Maisel Family

Bent over the tripod near Steamboat Springs, spring 2014
Photo courtesy of the Maisel Family

slanted, split roof of the Crain Communications Building, and Lake Michigan, on a hot, sunny day.

Max immersed himself in the art of photography at RIT, renowned for its curriculum in that field. In the winter of his sophomore year, he called me and very hesitantly asked if, on spring break, I would go with him to Steamboat; he had an idea for a photography class project. I knew enough about parenting to know that if your twenty-year-old asks you to spend time with him, you drop what you're doing and go spend time with him.

Again, I took pictures of him taking pictures. I have one of him, bent like a pipe cleaner at the waist, peering into the lens. The highlight of Max's trip may have been the afternoon he spent with Tudor, discussing photographic technique. Don couldn't have been more generous with his time and expertise. Max ate it up. He let down his guard and actively engaged with Don. I worked at a nearby table. Actually, I pretended to work, because I couldn't believe how chatty Max allowed himself to be. I texted Meg, "You wouldn't believe Max!"

A couple of weeks after Max disappeared, I contacted Don. I must have left him a voice message. When he called back, I remember telling him, and he said, "That's why I don't answer the phone. It's usually bad news."

The most important artifacts of the trip are the prints of the photos that Max took out there—blue skies framing snow-covered valleys and hills in the early spring, and a portrait of me. He needed me to sit for a class assignment. And I mean sit. I had to stay in the same position for thirty minutes while he wrestled the lights and got the camera in the right position. He forbade me from smiling—professor's order. That's a long time to sit stone-faced. Max didn't like to photograph people; it meant having to communicate with them. I was a safe harbor, yet even with me he fretted about every small detail. He had so little confidence. We learned after he died that, as much as he loved photography, he pursued it out of desperation. Max believed fine art photography to be the only major at RIT in which he could graduate. He wasn't an engineer; he wasn't a techie; he had no desire to pursue science or the liberal arts.

In fact, Max was succeeding at photography (Meg and I love the portrait that Max took of me). He just refused to grasp that. One of his professors, Frank Cost, took an active interest in Max, who reminded him of his middle child. Cost had shepherded him through one difficult class, so much so that Max became a dinner-table topic between him and his wife. Max struggled in the class, but then he figured it out, and over the last six weeks he shined. At the end of the semester, Cost singled out three students in the class for their work. Max was one of them.

Max took a second class from Cost, on aerial and drone photography, in the winter of 2015. He sat in the front and to the side, so he could see the whole classroom, and he never missed a session. He earned pocket money as a class notetaker, an important job at RIT, where about 1,200 students are deaf (I once suggested to Max that he learn American Sign Language so that he could talk to his deaf classmates. I thought it would be a way to meet people that might not intimidate him as much as talking did. I don't know why I thought that communicating with his hands might be easier for him than communicating with his mouth. I don't remember if he even responded to my suggestion.) When Max failed to take his customary seat in the front of the class on that last Tuesday of February, Cost told me and Meg that he immediately sensed something bad had happened. After Max died, Cost published a book in which he discussed Max, his work, and how Max's classmates

I sat for a portrait by Max during our trip to Steamboat Springs.
Photo credit: Max Maisel

came together in mourning. It is a marvelous, harrowing keepsake. There are photos of Max among the other students, photos taken by Max of class activities—Cost knew Max well enough to put him to work, ensuring that he was occupied by the task, not preoccupied by stress.

After Max died, Cost wrote to tell us of "the incredible diligence and hard work with which he approached every assignment I had ever given to him."

At the time Max disappeared, we knew little of this. Max had refused to show us any of his work, no matter how regularly we asked. Finally, on his last Hanukkah, after a direct maternal—request? command?—Max gave Meg a digital frame with forty landscapes. That slideshow ran in our family room, twenty-four hours a day, for months after Max died until the thing just gave out. I am usually the first one in the house to awaken, and when I went downstairs, Max's pixels seemed alive, bidding me good morning from him as they cast an ethereal, changing glow through the darkness.

When Meg and I arrived at RIT after he disappeared, we went to his on-campus apartment, campus police in tow. We found several boxes of large photo prints, class projects. We took the prints back to my brother-in-law's house in Rochester and laid out several of them on a long table for the family to enjoy. More than enjoy, really. I wanted his cousins, his aunts and uncles, his grandparents to see that he had a talent. His professors thought so.

That spring and summer, the RIT School of Photographic Arts and Sciences exhibited Max's work in the William Harris Gallery on campus. Seeing his work on display swelled our pride and crushed our hearts in equal proportion.

His photographs included a handful of self-portraits that illustrate his low self-regard. I am certain that left to his own devices, the last person Max would have photographed would have been Max. That may have been the most fascinating aspect of his love for photography—from an early age, Max viscerally objected to posing for a photo. We have photos of both my extended family and Meg's in which Max refused to look at the camera. With the Maisels he is in Meg's arms, turned around, facing the cousins standing behind him. With the Murrays he is standing next to his Opa, looking down, providing a good shot of the crown of his head.

I hesitate to read too much into his self-portraits taken for classes because I don't know what his professors assigned him to do.

One photo is of him standing in front of a mirror, reaching out to touch his reflection. His fingers barely reach the mirror. The tentative quality of the gesture lends itself to Max's appearance. He looks haunted, exhausted. His hair appears to have eluded both a brush and a bottle of shampoo for several days.

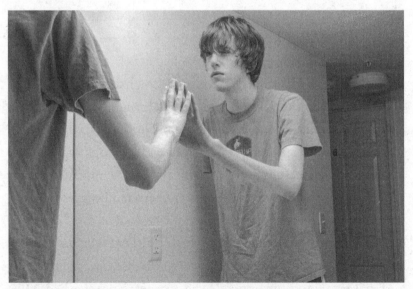

Part of Max's portfolio that RIT exhibited in its memorial tribute to him
Photo credit: Max Maisel

Another photo, taken in our basement, shows a shadow of Max on the left side, and a half exposure of him on the right. Included in the envelope with the print is his professor's assessment, which said in part, "I really like the image where you appear to be faded, but don't be so hard on yourself when you described yourself as a dull person and that is why you wanted to appear faded in the image."

There are millions of people who see the world as half empty whose view does not morph into mental illness. Besides, Meg and I both knew that inside the shell that Max built around himself lay a kernel of sweetness. Actually, not a kernel but a big, doughy lump. After Max died, we received a beautiful note from a woman who had grown up in our neighborhood. In her junior year of high school, when Sarah was nine, Max seven, and Elizabeth almost four, we took Katie on a family skiing vacation to help us wrangle the three of them. In her note, Katie described putting Max to bed. He asked her to tell him a story. He got into bed, and Katie sat on the edge and began her story. As she regaled him, Katie wrote, Max reached up and softly stroked her cheek. Katie went on to say that she had become a sixth-grade English teacher at a boys' school. One advisee, Katie wrote, "is a Minecraft lover who could out-strategize me in any logic puzzle or outthink me in any creative venture. He has some trouble interacting with his peers, but he instantly endeared himself to me and is now one of my most favorite. Maybe I see something in him from a little boy I knew years ago . . ."

I have a theory that skeptics are really idealists who form a shell of self-protection. That describes most journalists, and I think it describes Max. He was, in original form, a sweet soul, a side he felt free to display to our pets. I always believed that Max bonded with them because he could trust them emotionally, because what he saw was what he got. They didn't present him with the unsolvable mysteries he found in trying to connect with his peers.

He loved Cece but utterly devoted himself to Calvin, a black, long-haired barn cat. Max was ten when we adopted Cece, a five-year-old yellow lab, a few months before we picked up two kittens, which Max suggested we name after his favorite comic strip, *Calvin and Hobbes*. The latter lived only a few months. Meg and I decided to bury Hobbes in our backyard and have a funeral, so that the kids would understand the rituals of death and perhaps gain some closure. Max insisted on putting three items inside the shoebox coffin with Hobbes: a Lego character's hat, so that Hobbes would have a toy; a spinal key chain, so that Hobbes would always have an intact

Calvin, the love of Max's life and a regular camera subject. Note the portrait of sixteen-year-old Max on the wall behind Calvin.
Photo credit: Max Maisel

backbone; and a picture of Max, so that Hobbes always would remember him.

What's sweeter than that?

Max would drape Calvin around his neck, generally leaping at any opportunity to foist himself upon him. Calvin, hardly a lap cat, rarely rejected the attention. He tolerated it from the rest of us. He received it graciously from Max. On the rare occasion that we got a letter from Max at summer camp, he would sign off with, "I love you Calvin."

In the summer of 2014, Max stayed on campus at RIT, catching up on credits. At home, Calvin, nine years old, began suffering kidney failure. He stopped eating, and the veterinarian informed us that little could be done. We went to extraordinary lengths, financially and otherwise—let's just say I don't expect to give another pet twice-daily IVs—to keep Calvin alive until Max finished his semester and came home. Calvin made it for a few more days; his death hit Max so hard—he declined to come out in the yard when we buried Calvin—I wonder if it was his first step down the slide of depression.

By that time, Max had built thicker and thicker walls around his sweetness, walls thick with worry and frustration, disappointment, and his own stubbornness. If you've ever been a teenager, you recall how they feel about authority: you only want it when you need it. You're trying to assert your independence, even you understand as well as your parents do that you can no more handle true independence than you could a live tiger. And yet Max never strayed far from compliance. He recoiled at defying authority. He recoiled at most anything that daunted him. He pursued his driver's license when he turned eighteen only because Meg and I rebelled at driving him everywhere.

"Why should I do something for you that you can do yourself?" I told him.

Once he got his license—over the better judgment of his driver's ed instructor—Max was the rare, if not only, teenager in Fairfield who drove below the speed limit. One of our neighbor's kids came home one day and announced that half the neighborhood reported late to their first class that morning because they got behind Max going up the hill to campus.

We were so proud of Max for learning to overcome his fears and becoming competent enough to drive the seven hours from Fairfield to RIT by himself. I told him all the time, when he set his mind to it, he could do anything. Meg and I both believed that if Max could just get through high school, he would find his people in college, the way so many others have. Of course, Max didn't take the typical route to his peeps. Or maybe he did, as far as this generation is concerned.

When Max first went online, we gave him the parental spiel about not speaking with strangers over the internet. But during Max's teen years, he took his interests in manga, anime, and video games online. He began to play Minecraft with and against people all over the country. In this group, Max found his people. He played furtively because he thought he was breaking a parental rule. He played so furtively that he didn't tell us that he chose to attend RIT because he had online friends among the student body. A few weeks into his freshman year, Max wanted to attend an anime convention in Detroit with all these friends. His desire to go to Detroit conflicted with his desire to follow the rules. So he sent us a long email in the fall of his freshman year, explaining who these friends were and why he thought he should be able to go.

Meg and I couldn't have been happier. He had friends!

One of his online friends, a quiet, sweet, young woman from Houston whom I will call Shauna, became Max's first real love interest. Max and Shauna bonded online. Over one Christmas break, she came to our home in Connecticut, the first time they met in person. The two of them made a sweet couple. Their relationship lasted a year and a half, and the breakup really hurt Max. This struck me as entirely normal. First loves leave a scar. A breakup left me in a funk for most of my sophomore year of college. Max mostly suffered his heartbreak in silence. Max pretty much suffered everything in silence. He confided occasionally in his mother, his everlasting safe harbor, but her soothing love didn't calm him.

Toward the end of 2014, Max seemed to be emerging from his heartbreak. Shauna reappeared in his life and resumed, if not a relationship, a friendship. And yet he despaired. Despite his shyness, despite his lack of instinct for dealing with other people, Max hungered for connection, just as he had as a grammar-school boy at that neighborhood party. Don't we all? Two days before he ended his life, Max paid for a one-year subscription to OkCupid, the online dating site. When we first learned of this, we wondered how a mind bent toward suicide would make room for something so optimistic. And yet he reached the conclusion that his desire to love and be loved was a character flaw. That's not impatience, that's just not thinking clearly. We found this passage in his computer after his death.

> Selfish as it sounds—and even though I've been told by many that it isn't, it still feels like it is—I want a relationship. I want to be with someone again, to have that feeling of closeness that I had in the past. But nothing's working. I get paralyzed on the inside when I try to talk to a new person in person, and all of my attempts on okcupid have petered out and died within a day or so. That's how desperate

I've gotten—and even that's failed. I know people here care, and I know other internet friends care, but . . . it's not the same. It's not enough. And that's why I still feel selfish. Even though I have a lot going for me, I still want something more.

It's always easier to see the slide in retrospect than it is in real time. One of the enduring mysteries for me of Max's last weeks is how much he consciously hid his hopelessness from those who could help him, and how much of his unwillingness to seek or accept help emanated from the mental illness itself. He told his parents and his sisters very little. We knew he worried that he wouldn't be able to find a job or an internship for the upcoming summer between his junior and senior year. He openly fretted about it. After he disappeared, his career services advisor at RIT contacted us to describe her effort to help him calm his nerves. "During our appointment a couple of weeks ago," she said, "we worked on an introductory email for one of the photographers Max had selected (to send his resume). When Max hit 'send' on that email, he smiled and said, 'Well, that wasn't too bad,' and a slight grin replaced the intensity on his face."

While home for the holidays, Max told the psychologist he had seen regularly throughout his adolescence that his life was going well. When Max reached out for help at RIT, he left the campus counselor with the impression that he didn't intend to harm himself. Did he try to deceive? Did his mind whipsaw from hope to despair, from seeing a future to just wanting the pain to stop?

We didn't know until after Max died that he had reached out to the campus counseling center in the first week of February 2015. He had been wracked by grief. Max and his online friend group had been devoted to two online anime series, *Red v. Blue* and *RWBY* (pronounced "Ruby"), developed by Monty Oum, a young animator at Rooster Teeth, a production house in Austin. Max and his friends watched it, argued over it, and watched it again. On January 22, one week after Max turned twenty-one, Oum, thirty-three, suffered an allergic reaction during a medical procedure and went into a coma. He died on February 1. The *New York Times* reported on February 5 about the outpouring of grief among Oum's fans, quoting the actor LeVar Burton, whose daughter Mica was also in college at the time.

"When I arrived, she just fell into my arms, sobbing," Burton told the *Times*. He added that "the depth of grief was, and is, surprising."

Yeah, we can vouch for that. Max had been struggling, and Oum's death may have been the catalyst that launched Max into the slide from which he could not recover. Again, this is what we began piecing together after Max disappeared, the jigsaw puzzle that we continue to try to solve.

Two days after Oum died, Max went to see a campus psychiatrist. He had developed a hand tremor, most likely a side effect of his antidepressant. Max just couldn't get a break; on the list of least desirable side effects for a photographer, a hand tremor has got to be second to blindness. The campus psychiatrist prescribed a second medication to quell the tremor. There's a possibility that the two medications mixed so poorly that they helped propel Max into his irreversible decline. We found some evidence of the mixture going poorly on the internet. But we also know that Max had started to spiral before he ever received the second medication. Whatever he said to the psychiatrist concerned the doctor enough that he sent Max to the campus counseling center for an emergency session.

Speaking of finding puzzle pieces, much of what I am about to discuss we didn't know until the summer of 2018, when the psychologist who saw Max in his emergency session and the head of the campus counseling center agreed to meet with us. We believe that RIT wouldn't allow them to meet with us until the three-year statute of limitations for filing a suit against the university had elapsed. We had no interest in filing suit. Vengeance wouldn't bring Max back. The meeting lasted about an hour and a quarter, and it became clear to us that the mental health professionals at RIT remained haunted by how Max slipped through their fingers.

Max agreed to the emergency intervention, and in that session he told the psychologist that Oum's death made him want to disappear. He said specifically that he had thought of suicide. The psychologist asked if he had a plan for killing himself, and if he intended to act. The answers to those questions are the gauge by which counselors determine the severity of mental illness. Max gave the answers that turned off the alarm bells. He said he had decided it was too cold to act upon his plan. He said that he had class assignments that he needed to complete, that he still had experiences in his life that provided enjoyment. The psychologist asked him to come back the next day. They talked more extensively about his grief for Oum. They discussed hospitalization only long enough for Max to turn it down because, again, he had work to do. That is, from the standpoint of mental health, a good answer. He wanted to complete his academic assignments. That meant that he cared about his future. If you intend to end your life, what difference does your photographic classwork make?

The psychologist asked Max to come back the following week, on February 11. In that session Max agreed to engage in further talk therapy—again, a sign that he saw a future—and made an appointment for Tuesday, February 24. That, of course, is the morning after law enforcement informed us and RIT that Max's car had been found at Charlotte Pier. On that morning, a police officer waited in the campus counseling center for Max to appear for his appointment. By then, he had become a missing person. In fact, soon after Max had that February 11 appointment, the last one he attended, he began to plan the end of his life.

In our meeting, the psychologist filled in blanks for us. We filled in blanks for the psychologist. We felt enormously frustrated then, and still do now, that we had not been notified that he had told the doctor that he had suicidal thoughts. That may have been because Max, in the eyes of the law, had passed into adulthood. The psychologist assured us that had Max checked the box for *acting* upon his suicidal thoughts, we would have been contacted. But the head of the counseling service also made us understand that that decision is not made lightly. The doctors understand that if they treat the students as someone's child instead of as the adult that the law says they are, it may come at the cost of the students' trust.

I understand the tricky, professional balance. I understand that the university is in a difficult position. I understand that in loco parentis went out of fashion in higher education decades ago. But I also understand that if the first priority is the well-being of the student, then I believe that the psychologist, the counseling service, and the university all failed Max.

The meeting never strayed much beyond information swapping. I don't know what the protocol is for mental health professionals when their treatment goes awry. I suppose they try to find solace the way the rest of us do. They have so few people with whom they can discuss their loss, both personally and professionally. Their questions, like ours, go unanswered. A few days after our meeting, the psychologist sent us an email, explaining how Max's death remained haunting, confusing. The Max who walked out of the counseling office on February 11 seemed to have a ray of hope, to begin to emerge from his grief. And yet within two weeks he decided to walk down that pier.

It has not escaped me that I am writing about what I learned of grief, and that grief, specifically Max's grief for Oum, helped catapult him toward his demise. Grief overwhelmed Max, yes, but it did so at a moment when his defenses already lay in tatters. Max would have been ill equipped to handle grief even if he hadn't been suffering. Max rarely opened a window into his interior life—he rarely opened a window into his exterior life. Max was emotionally immature. He walled himself off from most deep emotions in an effort at self-protection. Max believed that if he allowed himself to have hope, he would just set himself up for disappointment. "You could tell he was somebody who felt things in a really big way," the psychologist told us.

When grief confronted Max, he internalized it. He did when our pets died. He did when my father died. What I knew of his emotional pain I heard secondhand from his mother, and she didn't hear a lot. On his last return home, the holiday break in December 2014 / January 2015, Meg took Max to dinner one night at a burger joint in downtown Fairfield. As they chatted, she began probing.

"We want you to be happy," Meg said.

"I know you and Dad accept me for who I am," Max replied.

"Yes, of course we do," Meg said, "because we love you. You know that?"

He knew that. That conversation provided solace in the weeks and months (and years) after he ended his life, even as neither Meg nor I have brought ourselves to set foot in that particular burger joint again. Max left no note, which the police also said we should take as a blessing. A note left by a suicide victim is a snapshot of someone consumed by mental illness. The victim may assess blame or say something hurtful, both of which leave an emotional wound that could take years to heal. It's understandable how the impact of a final note might overwhelm the evidence of the life that preceded it.

Max didn't leave a note, and he told Meg that he knew we accepted him and loved him. Phew. I had enough to process on my own.

As someone masterful in the art of emotional avoidance, I glided around Max's issues as smoothly as Wayne Gretzky at center ice, puck on his stick. In retrospect, it devastates me to say that I built the bridges for him to walk to my interests—comedy, movies, basketball—yet I rarely crossed over onto his terrain. I am sure I am not the first parent of my generation who failed to grasp the saliency of a Pokémon deck, the intricacies of navigating the latest Super Mario adventure on Game Boy, or the musical genius that is the video game soundtrack. That's what Max downloaded onto his iPod.

I am smart enough to know that had I dived into any of those, rather than pretend to have a passing interest, it would have had no bearing on his mental illness. I thought my role had to be parent, not friend. But I am haunted by the isolation that Max felt, and I think I could have done more to quell it. I am haunted by how desperately I cling to the memory of one NBA game we attended, a New Jersey victory over Cleveland in game 3 of the 2007 Eastern Conference Semifinal. Max, thirteen, and I sat twenty rows behind a basket. When one of the Nets—Jason Kidd? Vince Carter?—clinched the game from the free-throw line, Max and I embraced and began jumping up and down.

Why the memory of that one moment means so much to me does not put me in a flattering light. I love it because that is the most vivid moment of Max fulfilling those assumptions I so naively made before he came to be. That may have been the moment he most closely resembled a sports fan. It underlines the difficulty I encountered reaching him on his terms. It makes me think that at some level, I lived in denial of his problems, a denial partly rooted in my genuine faith that he would ultimately succeed, and mostly rooted in my fear of admitting to myself how desperate his mental condition might be.

Emotional avoidance, take a bow.

Later in his life—late in his life, as it turned out—as the weight of his depression rested more heavily on Max's bony frame, I rarely discussed it with him. I didn't want to bring it up, didn't want to acknowledge it. It took me years to realize that my attitude toward his troubles parrots the attitude toward grief that so many people exhibited to me and Meg after Max died, the attitude that galvanized me to write this book.

I didn't want to make my fear of Max's illness affect him. Once Max died, I found myself on his side of the equation, dealing with people who didn't want to bring up my grief because of their discomfort. It dawned on me that I failed to address Max's depression in any meaningful way. I do not believe that my acknowledgment to him of his depression might have put him on the road to improvement. Mental illness is more insidious than that, more impervious to manipulation. But I might have comforted him. I might have empathized with him. I didn't.

My life didn't stop when Max died. It changed in a gut-wrenching, horrible, so very sad way, yes. But my life didn't stop. I enjoyed the luxury of stepping around grief for the first fifty-five years of my life. It is an emotion that I simply refused to acknowledge, at significant cost to me and my family. I was scared of grief. I was scared of the grieving. And then, without warning, I was immersed in it.

Chapter Four

Going Public

I don't consider myself a public figure. I am on television occasionally. I am best known in my native South, where college football is neck and neck with Southern Baptist for most popular religion. I live in the Northeast, where the only way you could make college football a religion is if the Yankees and Red Sox ditch the American League for the Big Ten.

But because I worked at ESPN, and since I appeared on television occasionally, when Max disappeared, it was not just the story of a college student gone missing. This story had a hook to it, and the hook went right into my cheek: The *son of an ESPN writer* went missing. Just the right intoxicant for online readers.

Max always hated being the center of attention. One of the smiles we allowed ourselves in those darkest days came in thinking of how he would have felt about trending on Twitter or being a story on *People* magazine's website.

I realized Max had become a story. We had become a story. Believe me when I tell you I didn't care. I had bigger things on my mind, like putting one foot in front of the other, like dealing with the detectives working on land, like watching the police scuba team troll the icy shallows of the Great Lake that probably held our son. Not to mention that the journalistic instincts of a thirty-four-year career forbade me from stonewalling the media. I didn't want to "no comment" anyone. Writers and broadcasters want to tell a story. If you help us tell your story, we'll treat you well. Or at least fairly.

None of this was front and center in my brain in the first seventy-two hours. It is more of a baseline picture of how I think, which I am explaining to set the scene for the epiphany that enabled me to grieve openly.

Meg and I spent that first night calling Rochester hospitals, trying to spin out scenarios of where he might be. It took Meg a couple of days to wrap her head around the notion that Max might have died. She was sure he would turn up, and she was sure she would give him hell for putting us through this when he did.

We didn't sleep much that night. Shortly after daylight, Meg, Elizabeth, and I threw clothes in the car and drove the seven hours to Rochester. On the drive up, we began to spread the word among our siblings and parents. Meg's three brothers and four sisters began driving, from Cincinnati and northern Virginia, from New Hampshire and Maine and Syracuse. My brother and sister and my nieces and nephews, none of whom lived north of Atlanta or west of New Orleans, dropped their lives and began making their way to the frozen north.

As if Max's disappearance didn't put enough on our plate, during the drive Elizabeth began having stomach pains so severe that upon arriving in Rochester, I took her to the emergency room. It turned out to be some sort of bacterial infection. I remember the surreality of her sitting on an exam table, the local cable news station droning on the TV above us, and seeing Max's picture on the screen. The news played on a thirty-minute loop; we were there maybe three hours. I know we saw the news report several times. I remember pointing to it and saying to a nurse, "That's my son, her brother. That's why we are here." It's hard to make an emotional dent in an emergency room nurse. I think that did.

(The following month, Elizabeth had an appointment to have her wisdom teeth extracted. On the consulting visit a few days before, the oral surgeon went over everything with me and Elizabeth. It hit me that she would have to be anesthetized. One of my two remaining children was having an operation. Before Max died, I took medical expertise for granted. Not anymore, and especially not so soon after losing Max. When the doctor finished, I pointed at her, stared him down, and said, in a quavery voice, "Her brother died three weeks ago. *Don't fuck this up.*" The doctor's eyes widened, and he said something about operating on his own daughter, and that he operated on every patient as if it were his daughter. Everything went fine.)

The memories I have of those first hours and days after Max disappeared are not so much blurry as they are scattered; staccato; at best, snapshots.

Two of our closest friends, Tom Reilly and Linda Barlaam, immediately hopped in a car to make the 360-mile drive to tend to us for a couple of days, kindnesses we will never forget.

For three days, the Rochester police cast doubts on the supposition that Max died an intentional death. Max did not check the boxes of people who end their own lives. The detectives suggested more than once that perhaps Max had ditched his car and gone off on what the Aussies call a walkabout. Max wouldn't have been the first college student to do so. But Meg and I knew that Max hadn't disappeared in a good way. For one thing, as I explained, Max was a rule follower. He wouldn't have just left. For another, the friends of his that we knew of at RIT were all present and accounted for. Many of them also belonged to Max's online community; we couldn't find someone anywhere who could tell us where Max might have gone. And yet another indication of distress: Meg checked his credit card purchases and his RIT food service account. He had stopped buying meals a few days before he disappeared.

On the fourth day of our lakeside vigil, as we arrived at the docks on one more gray and brutally cold February evening, one of the detectives pulled me and Meg aside. He asked us to put the girls in the car. He wanted to speak to us alone.

"I have some news," he said. The cops had begun some forensic work on Max's computer and credit card records and found evidence that he intended to harm himself.

So there it was.

We thanked the detective. We thanked the scuba team chief when he came off the lake to tell us they hadn't found Max. On our one-mile drive back to where we were staying, Meg suggested we not say anything to anyone in our families about the news that gave form to our worst suspicions. She wanted time to process the information, to figure out what to say. But I didn't understand that. I didn't ask her how long she needed. I just nodded.

We numbly followed our extended families as we descended en masse on a Thai restaurant. I say numbly because I don't like Thai food. That's how numb I was—I went to a Thai restaurant. I sat at one end of a long table of Murrays and Maisels. There was a lot of talk—you should meet our families—little of it by me. Something bothered me, and I couldn't figure out how to articulate it. Even when we stopped afterward at Abbott's, a frozen custard place that made Max very happy, I cut short any of my family's attempts at conversation with me. My memory is of almost feeling physically uncomfortable in my skin.

As we drove back to the house, as I stared out the window at the Rochester tundra, it dawned on me what was eating at me.

I don't like keeping secrets.

Losing Max was burden enough. I didn't want the secret of how he died to weigh on me as well. The last thing I wanted to do was have to keep track of which members of our families knew what. That sounded like unnecessary work, not to mention the emotional issues that would bloom as our extended family discovered that some knew all and all knew only some.

Meg didn't feel any differently. She just needed some time. But I didn't have the patience to wait. I didn't want to return to the house and for one more second keep what we knew from our families. It was hard enough for me to carry my end of a conversation as it was.

As everyone walked into the house and started shedding winter layers, I pulled Meg aside.

"I can't do this," I said. "I can't not tell them what we know."

We told our girls, and then we gathered everyone in the living room. I stood in the middle, surrounded by the people who love us more dearly than anyone else, who raced to what felt like the coldest place on earth (on that day, the low in Rochester was 1 degree) because we needed them. I stuffed my hands in my back pockets. When I began to speak, I kept my eyes focused on the ground. If I had looked at anyone, I would have choked up. And I said to our families what became the foundational tenet of my grieving.

"We have never been ashamed of Max," I said. "And we're not going to start now. This is what we found out today."

I had come to the realization that I had to take the lead, that I had to be the shepherd in tone of how we as an extended family responded, both privately and publicly. You have to understand: I am the youngest of three children. I grew up being told what to do by parents and siblings. I always looked to others for guidance. But in these moments, I grasped that Meg and I knew more about this heartbreak than anyone in our extended families. We could depend on them for support, for succor, for love. They had our backs. But they had our backs because we were out-front.

So I laid out the framework of what the detective told us.

By not being secretive, we didn't add to our considerable burden.

By not being secretive, we didn't act as if Max's death deserved secrecy. The first rule of stigma is that it's a badge of something to which you don't want to be attached.

By not being secretive, if someone thought Max's death was shameful, or if someone didn't want to participate in a conversation about Max, that would be their burden. I hope that's not inconsiderate. I don't mean it that way. To this day, I don't broadcast how my son died. I don't shy away from it, either. I play a lot of golf, and, invariably, when playing with someone I don't know well, the conversation on the walk down the fairway turns to children.

"How many kids do you have?"

I make sure to modulate my tone. I don't mumble. I don't speak with an air of apology for answering an unloaded question with an emotional blast. The only hurt I suffer is that I don't answer, as I did for twenty-one years, in chronological order.

"We have two girls, twenty-nine and twenty-four," I say, "and our son died six years ago. He was twenty-one, a junior in college. He went into a spiral, and we didn't know it, and he ended his life."

That answer always elicits a gasp; it's the words that follow the gasp that provide a gauge of how my explanation landed. Pretty much everyone gets out an "I'm sorry." They usually don't venture much beyond that. I wish they did. I am willing to answer any questions about Max as simply and matter-of-factly as I answer the first one. You asked about my children. Max remains one of my children. Not only for my own peace of mind, but for the greater good. The fact is, mental illness needs sunlight. Suicide makes people uncomfortable. Only recently has it begun to emerge as a topic spoken only after pulling someone aside, and then in a whisper. But I will talk about it. I am not ashamed of it. We as a family need to talk about it for reasons of catharsis. We as a society need to talk about it, very simply, to save lives. Not just the lives of those considering it but the quality of lives of those whom suicide leaves behind. I came to believe that the four of us, and everyone who rushed to the ramparts with support, emotional and caloric, would survive this wound. It would leave a scar. How disfiguring and disabling the scar became would be up to us.

To be clear, on the night that I spoke to our extended family, the larger meaning of grieving openly about Max's death escaped me. But the principle remained at the core of why Meg and I decided to make our grief public. Not only that, the manner in which our families responded reinforced our instincts. No one blinked. My oldest sibling Kathy has kept an eye out for her baby brother my entire life. She is the definition of warmth and unflappability, constantly doing for our mom, her four children, and her seven grandchildren. In the autumn of 2010, Kathy's husband Mike died unexpectedly at age sixty, shortly before their thirty-fourth wedding anniversary. Kathy had an inkling of what awaited us. In Rochester, she pulled Meg aside, looked her straight in the eye, and said, "Meg, sometimes, shitty things happen." Meg and I both appreciated the straightforwardness and understood Kathy's message. You are going to have to accept this.

After I finished speaking to the families, all of us on both sides—the northeastern Catholics and the southern Jews—opened our hearts. The wake and sitting shiva have a lot in common. Those who love the mourning family rush to comfort its members with companionship. The Jews subtract the open casket—we didn't have Max's body yet, anyway—and, as with most Jewish ritual events, add copious amounts of food to soak up the alcohol.

We sat there for a couple of hours, aunts, uncles, and cousins, telling Max stories. That night remains the warmest moment in the worst week of my life. Max's death set into motion so much transformation for me, Meg, Sarah, and Elizabeth. We had to figure out how to accommodate the gaping absence in our lives. For instance, I remember being devastated by the notion that we were no longer "the five of us." We—this family that Meg and I had created and nurtured since we married twenty-six years earlier—had become "the four of us." Four seemed like a comb-over, like we were pretending to look like a family, trying to camouflage what we no longer had. I felt like we had become an amputee, and there is no prosthesis available.

The same for how I refer to our children. They went from "the kids" to "the girls." That still stings.

So "the girls" and I returned home to Fairfield on Sunday. Meg stayed in Rochester, maintaining our vigil, going to the pier, being available for police and the scuba team trying to find Max. We arrived in a community waiting to envelop us in love. Trees up and down the streets of our neighborhood were wrapped with red ribbons; a flier with Max's photo and the caption "MISSING" was taped in the glass door of the corner newsstand. A couple of days earlier there had been a gathering at our temple, attended by people of many faiths. On that very morning, a local church said prayers for Max.

I dropped Sarah and Elizabeth off at the house and drove up to the corner to fill up the car. I stood at the gas tank on a raw, gray, late-winter day, not wanting to see anyone, not wanting to speak to anyone, and my neighbor Tom Wilkinson walked up with his dog. Tom is a union official, a nice guy with steel in his spine. Tom didn't see me right away. But then his eyes locked on me, and as he and the dog walked toward the car, I thought, hooboy, here we go. How awkward is this going to be?

"Ivan!" he said. "Jesus Christ! What the fuck?"

Not exactly Walt Whitman, but exactly what I needed to hear. I didn't want touchy-feely. I didn't want to deal with someone who didn't know what to do, who didn't know what to say. Hell, I didn't know what to do or say, either. Someone else saw the absurdity, the surreal nature of how our lives had turned upside down in the past six days.

I got back to the house and called Debra, my therapist. We had heard from her when Max disappeared.

"Well," I said, "do you want us to come to your office, or would you just like to move into our house?"

We awoke on Monday and, in one of the dumber decisions in the history of parenting, I talked Elizabeth into going back to school. Connecticut law states that if a senior has eighteen absences, that student may not receive a diploma. Elizabeth had just missed four days the previous week. She was going to have to miss more at some point. Just go on the first day, I said. It's going to be awful, get it out of the way, climb back onto the horse, et cetera. I thought that even as I actually wrote in my laptop that day, "I don't want to work." I thought that even as we walked to the front door of the high school and I asked her, "Who has the bigger pit in their stomach—me or you?"

Yes, Elizabeth acquiesced and went to her morning classes. The image she described of everyone staring at her in the hallway between classes haunts me to this day. Every time I think of it, I apologize to her.

I performed the same dumb service for Sarah. When she decided to quit her job so she could stay with us indefinitely, I tried to make sure she understood the consequences. She understood the priorities better than I did. "I'll never be scared of anything again," she said. If she could make it through losing her brother, she wouldn't begin to fret over leaving her job.

Here's what haunts me about those anecdotes. Any mistakes I made with the girls recede into my memory with all the other interactions I have had with them. They are replaced by new interactions and, assuredly, by new parenting mistakes. When Max died, not only did I realize that there will be no new interactions, but the mistakes I made take on a sinister tone. I wondered whether they contributed to his decision to end his life. That is logical, if nonsensical. He was sick. But right about then two people reached out to help me and my family, two people who provided safe harbor we so dearly needed.

Jim Coyne, the principal at the high school, brought me and Elizabeth into his office. We sat down at a round table. He looked at us. He is a soft-spoken man, almost taciturn, but he cares deeply about his students and Elizabeth, in particular, for one heartbreaking reason.

"I lost a daughter to suicide," he said and looked up at the clock on his wall as if to measure the time since her death, "fifteen years ago."

Mr. Coyne told us not to worry about absences, not to worry about graduation, not to worry about anything. Elizabeth had an academic record that would make the angels sing. He told her, basically, come back to school when you're ready. If all you can do is make it to lacrosse practice, that's all you can do.

Elizabeth didn't go to class again for five weeks.

The other person who leapt to our aid, Robin Gurwitch, is a psychologist on the faculty at the Duke University School of Medicine. Robin and I grew up together, and our mothers maintained a close friendship for more than sixty years. Robin was teaching at Oklahoma State when terrorists bombed the Murrah Federal Building in Oklahoma City in 1995. She emerged from that tragedy as one of the nation's leading experts on helping children who have suffered traumatic experiences build resilience and coping skills. I hadn't talked to Robin since childhood; my phone rang, and we talked for ninety minutes as if we had just spoken the week before. Robin told me a few things that made a world of difference.

"It's probably no comfort," she said, "but there's zero, zero, zero, zero chance you could stop it. If somebody decides that's something they want to do, there is nothing that is going to get in their way short of them calling you up and saying, 'At 8:03 on Tuesday, I'm going to do this.' Nothing that you can do to prevent it. If you go to a mental health professional that tells you he can prevent that, don't go to him. You can't prevent it, and you can't predict it."

Robin referred to "the assumptive nature of life," everything unfolding as expected. I loved that phrase. I had a definition to explain that feeling I had for fifty-five years that tragedies happened to other people. Now that I had my own tragedy, she told me to attempt to parse Max's actions at my own peril.

"The reality is," Robin said, "we will never understand the reason and I hope we never do. It's not how our minds work."

I respond to logical explanations. For what it's worth, I don't believe in conspiracies. My professional life as a journalist has convinced me that most people can't keep their mouths shut long enough to pull off a surprise party, much less the sort of nonsense spouted from the far ends of the political spectrum. What Robin explained to me made sense. We think rationally. At the end, Max didn't. Maybe he was just exhausted. In the best of times, communicating with people was a minefield for him. One of his friends told Meg that Max had withdrawn from them, too. It unnerved Meg, and we wished any one of his friends had expressed whatever concerns they had about Max to us. But as we discussed it, we agreed that it would take an unusually mature college kid to reach out to the parents of a struggling friend. We knew Max well, and *we* didn't have the context to recognize the symptoms of mental illness. We couldn't be surprised that his friends didn't put two and two together, either.

Maybe Max felt he had nowhere to land. Maybe he just got tired. I wasn't any less sad. But I used Robin's logic to move past guilt, to move past bewilderment. As with all medicine, as with all therapy, your mileage may vary.

I began talking to Max, wherever he was, soon after the girls and I returned from Rochester. Meg talked to him all the time. She still does. I never spoke to him as often as she. But I do remember, the first time, groping for the right thing to say. I started to say, "I hope you didn't suffer." But when drowning yourself in 38-degree water is the escape you choose from your troubles, it's clear that you already are suffering. It gutted me to know that's how much he had suffered.

That's one example of the emotional torrent I faced, and as they used to say with box tops and baseball cards, collect them all. My conversation with Robin helped prepare me, but I was a guy who had stiff-armed emotion for most of my life. Here it came, and right away.

On a rainy, bone-chilling morning walk with our elderly lab, Cece, I saw our neighbor Kevin. When Max needed a job in high school, Kevin and his wife Denise hired Max to walk their springer spaniel Rudy every afternoon after school. Max was so responsible, so conscientious. Not to mention that he loved "the Rudester," as he called him. My memory of Max walking Rudy never fails to make me smile. Rudy had no leash discipline. He roamed everywhere, leash taut behind him, skinny, spindly Max at the other end, holding on for dear life.

Kevin and Denise had been there when Max needed them. I saw Kevin, and I just sagged into his arms. I began crying, Kevin began kissing the outside of the hoodie I wore in the rain, repeating, "I love you."

When Max was a little boy, one of our neighbors presented him with a tiny carved white elephant. Look at the top joint of your ring finger; that elephant would fit from there to fingertip. But it also fit snugly in the grip of a toddler. Max carried that elephant everywhere. When he lost it, we went to hell and back to find it. OK, maybe not hell, but Meg did jump into a muddy pond at her family's cottage at Charleston Lake, Ontario, to find it. We did return ten miles to a gas station convenience store in Deposit, New York. We did go back to a gas station in Fairfield, where it had fallen out of the car. Someone had placed it next to the pump. A parent, I suppose.

Max moved on from the elephant about the time he entered kindergarten, but Meg and I didn't. She had put it for safekeeping in a wooden jewelry box my parents gave Max when he became a

Bar Mitzvah. The jewelry box sat on top of the six-foot bookcase in Max's room. One of the first things Meg did when she returned home from Rochester was walk into Max's room, bring the jewelry box down, and pull out the elephant. Seeing it for the first time in years brought a flood of warm feelings. She looked at me and said, "You are not going to get to have it anytime soon." Now the elephant would be her talisman.

I had Max's tallit, the prayer shawl that adult Jews wear to any service in which the Torah is read. On my first Sabbath home, I wore it to services. I am not a regular attendee, to put it lightly, but I went thinking it would help me and that if I didn't go to services and say the mourning prayer of remembrance for Max, my dad would be upset. He had been dead for more than seven years, but I couldn't be too careful. Removing the tallit from its zippered case, I thought of my dad for another reason. In the later years of my parent's marriage, when they went to dinner, my dad would take the check, pull out his wallet, take out a $100 bill, and say to Mom, "This is all I have. You pay the check." This happened so often, my family began to assume it was the same $100 bill. We started to call it "Lonesome Ben" and tell stories about how Franklin would blink when he emerged briefly into the light.

Max's tallit saw sunlight about as often as Dad's C-note. When I wear that tallit, I think of Max, of my dad, of Lonesome Ben. You take your solace where you can find it.

The day that I found solace by driving two towns over to go to the grocery store, my day of magical shopping, wouldn't be the only pretending I did. In my day-to-day, moment-to-moment existence, Max hadn't been in the house regularly since he enrolled at RIT two and a half years earlier. It could very easily feel like he was still at school.

It might be a moment. It might be a few moments. And then reality would crash through my idyll.

A couple of days later, Meg went back to Rochester. The police had told us they would search for two weeks. They searched for three. She wanted to be there when they decided to call it off.

It was a Monday morning. "I think I will see you on Wednesday," she said.

"I think you're right," I said. "I'm sorry."

People believed we lived in agony because of the prolonged search for Max's body. It's hard to say. I had never had a son die and disappear before. Yes, had Max followed the template, and his body appeared three weeks earlier, then maybe we would be less anguished. But we had nothing to compare those three weeks with.

On Tuesday, March 16, the police called off the search. Spring approached. We would have to wait until the warming waters of Lake Ontario decided to surrender our son. We scheduled a memorial service for the following Friday, March 27.

Chapter Five

A Bad Day, a Great Ending

That last Friday in March may have been five weeks after Max disappeared, but it was the earliest we could have held a memorial service, or whatever it is you call a service when you don't have a body. We didn't want to plan anything until the scuba team found Max or stopped its search. Once the team suspended the search, we waited ten days in order to hold the service on a Friday, when it would be easier for our out-of-town friends and our extended families to come.

And come they did: family from across the country; college friends of mine, Meg, and Sarah, from California; work friends and former neighbors from Dallas; dozens of colleagues from ESPN, nearly an hour away; and Max's friends from RIT and his online community. Our entire lives gathered before us, somewhere around a thousand people arriving at our temple. I look back on their response in amazement; at the time, I was too numb to fully appreciate it.

I could control how I reacted to Max's disappearance; as I learned, probably a little too well. But the reactions of our friends as I saw them for the first time after Max disappeared gutted me. Either the emotion they felt for us unleashed what I buried, or, more likely, I reacted to their feelings for me, for us. It felt like bank-shot emoting, the loss of Max reflected through various prisms. But once I saw anyone for the first time, I got over that emotional hump. The only thought I remember constantly choking me up involved how my dad would have reacted. I have told you how direct he could be, and yet his love for his children and grandchildren (especially Max, I always believed) was so all-encompassing that I believe losing Max would have flattened my dad. I felt relief every time I thought about not having to call and tell him.

We settled into an existence, such as it was. I remember the girls being on the couch, under blankets, watching TV together. I think we watched every episode of *The Gilmore Girls* seventy-three times. Complete vegging. Sometimes the girls' friends came over. Meg and I joined them often, getting up to answer the door to accept food from neighbors or to invite in someone making a condolence call. None of us wore anything that had ever seen an iron. I remember wearing Max's winter shirts—big, thick, buffalo plaids and solid woolens from Filson. There's a story about those shirts.

I am the son of a clotheshorse. We used to joke that every upscale men's store in the nation had a picture of my father on the bulletin board in the salesmen's break room. Late in Dad's life, we went to Chicago for a family wedding. I remember walking into the men's department at Saks Fifth Avenue on the Miracle Mile, and a salesman hollered out, "Mr. Maisel!" He wasn't talking to me. Turns out the guy had sold Dad some clothes in South Florida years before.

My wardrobe paled before my father's, but he passed on his appreciation for fine menswear. Max, as I said earlier, didn't like wearing shirts with buttons. He didn't wear a tie unless someone in the family got married. But I still brought him into my closet and explained clothes to him. I still tried to bring him along with me when I shopped. One reason his decision to attend RIT thrilled me is that Rochester is the birthplace of Hickey Freeman, one of the finest old-line names in menswear. Hickey Freeman closed its Rochester factory years ago, but the company still ran an outlet store in the basement of the factory. I dragged Max there, too.

He and I found common ground in those Filson shirts. They may not have been dressy, but Max recognized their quality and liked how they looked on him, even though he usually wore them as shirt jackets over a long-sleeved tee. For the rest of that interminable winter-spring, and for much of the next one, I wore Max's Filson shirts. I still wear them occasionally. They maintain a connection from my late father to my late son.

What energy and focus Meg had she poured into making the memorial service not only meaningful but a true reflection of Max. She wanted live music to commemorate him and had the inspiration to arrange for two members of the Fairfield University Glee Club, Robert Schwartz and Benjamin Bayers, to perform the three songs she selected: "You'll Never Walk Alone," "Bridge over Troubled Water," and, in closing, "Let It Be." Our rabbi expressed some concern over Paul McCartney's reference to "Mother Mary," but we assured him that referred to the mother of Paul, not the mother of Christ. Meg also employed a 2005 recording of "To Make You Feel My Love," performed by Mick McAuley and Winifred Horan. Their version of Bob Dylan's song is lovely and haunting, and it helped carry Meg through our darkest days.

I focused on writing the eulogy for Max, although Meg helped with that, too. I needed the help. As I wrote, I found myself with a conundrum. When someone with a typical life span dies, we eulogize them with a few hundred words. Max barely made it to twenty-one, yet a few hundred words seemed insufficient to the task of capturing him. Perhaps if he had been more outgoing, I wouldn't have felt the frantic need to tell people about him. The four of us wanted to say so much. It felt so important that we define Max. We didn't want his illness and his public death to overshadow the son and brother we loved.

The girls each wrote their own eulogy. I didn't help, beyond reading and a little light editing when they finished. The one thing I did do: as they prepared their texts, I asked each of them to listen as I read my 2,500 words aloud. I had two goals in mind. I needed the practice, to deliver the eulogy smoothly, to prepare myself for the inevitable emotional moments. More important, I wanted them to hear my attempt to be open. We didn't need to shy away from telling anecdotes, from trying to entertain. I didn't envision my son's eulogy as a nightclub act. But the only thing anyone remembers about a boring message is the boredom.

Between the demands of grief and the logistics of preparing the service, it took all the energy that Meg and I had to get through the day at hand. But we did try to reserve extra attention for Elizabeth. Late March is when universities began rendering their admissions verdicts. She had been accepted to several schools, but Elizabeth wanted more than anything to go to Stanford, my and Sarah's alma mater. Elizabeth had decided she wanted to go to Stanford before she even began high school. Throughout high school, she busted her ass to prepare. She knew it was necessary: in our unhinged higher education system, she would be one of 42,487 applicants for the class of 2019. Stanford accepted 2,144. That's 1 in 20, for those of you scoring at home. Stanford announced that it would release its decisions on Tuesday, April 1.

Except Stanford didn't. It dawned on us that, five years earlier, Sarah had received her acceptance several days before the official announcement date, on the previous Friday at 6 p.m., eastern time. The Stanford admissions office shrewdly emailed the decisions and then went home for the weekend, thinking that two and a half days would cool the anger of the 95 percent of the high school seniors whom the university told, "It's not you. It's me." Not to mention the anger of the alumni parents who had faithfully supported the university for years with the expectation that their donations might wedge the crack in the door a little wider. We looked at the calendar and figured out that the decisions likely would arrive on the previous Friday, March 27—the day of the memorial service.

Well, I thought, that's probably good. Perhaps the backdrop of Max's memorial service would provide Elizabeth the perspective that usually comes only with adulthood. If she got turned down by Stanford, it wouldn't even be the worst thing that happened to her that day. I hoped for acceptance, but a 5 percent rate? Who banks on that?

By the day before the service, the sadness that had settled over the house like a marine layer had been pushed out by the loving energy of family and friends. Sarah's college mates arrived from across the country. So did mine. Meg's Cornell friends, who provided her remarkable support and love for months, arrived in droves. Our extended families arrived. We had so much emotional support, all of it needed. On Friday morning, we donned our uniforms—nice clothes, talismans (I wore one of Max's watches; Meg wore another), frozen smiles, distant stares—and went to our temple. The families stayed in a side lobby off the sanctuary as people began to arrive. I walked out there for some reason and saw colleagues from the *Dallas Morning News*, which I had left two decades before. I didn't know they were coming. I was so touched that I stopped and chatted with them. Other guests came to say hello, and it began to feel a little too much like a social gathering for my wounded psyche. I retreated to the side lobby.

When the top of the hour arrived. Meg and I followed the girls into the sanctuary. The space where we had been waiting—hiding, really—opened into the middle of the room. I knew it would be crowded. But this was two stops past crowded. The curtains at the back of the sanctuary had been opened onto the social hall. Hundreds of folding chairs back there had been filled, too.

We walked right through a section filled with my ESPN colleagues. I remember seeing people I had no idea were coming—not only network president John Skipper, who lived fifteen minutes away, but Tom Rinaldi from New Jersey, Matt Millen from Pennsylvania, Trevor Matich from Tennessee, Desmond Howard from Florida—and being momentarily gobsmacked. I'm telling you that to wow you not with their celebrity but their caring. Theirs are the faces that first caught my eye.

After all the planning, all the logistics, after our families had arrived, after we donned our funereal armor, after we filed into the temple sanctuary and walked down the aisle with nearly two thousand eyes on us, after we sat down in the front right pew, for the first time the surrealism of the occasion revealed itself.

Meg and I were sitting at our son's funeral.

I turned to my right and said softly in her ear, "Can you fucking believe this?"

When we got in bed that night, Meg told me that was the best thing anyone said to her all day.

The service went smoothly. The four of us went to the pulpit together. Meg knew herself well enough to know that she couldn't have made it through a eulogy of her own without breaking down, so she performed a nifty piece of deflection. She spoke for nearly five minutes, turning the attention of the audience back onto itself. She asked nine groups of people in our lives to stand, one by one, and remain standing: our extended families, Max's RIT and gaming friends, our neighborhood, the middle/high school communities, Sarah's and Elizabeth's friends who had come from near and far, our college friends, our friends from when we had lived in New York and Dallas, my ESPN family, and our local friends. As each group stood, the cumulative effect of involving everyone who had come to support us exponentially increased the emotional impact. Years later, one of my ESPN colleagues volunteered to me that is what he remembered the most about the service.

Sarah spoke first and got more than a few laughs by revealing her brother through anecdotes. In discussing his limited diet:

"He loved pizza bagels but hated pizza," Sarah said, "until he figured out that pizza bagels were mini-pizzas. Then, in Max logic, he decided he didn't like pizza bagels.

"He loved sour candy and hated sharing it. In car trips, Elizabeth and I would always open our purchases as soon as we left the gas station. We'd always offer our goods to Max in the hopes that he'd reciprocate.

"But his answer was always the same: 'When I open it'—and this could be three hours later.

"When he finally did open his bag or box, you can bet he would give you one or two pieces of candy. Stingy. Annoying when he had sour watermelons. Downright cruel when he had Nerds and would legitimately give you one pellet of candy because, well, 'You asked for *one*.'"

As Sarah finished the comedy routine, her voice began to shake. She persevered through the tears. Our kids grew up during the time when the biggest event of their summers was the release of the next Harry Potter novel. Sarah recalled how, even as teenagers, the two of them missed a highway exit on a road trip because they were so engrossed in an audiobook.

"Lately," Sarah closed, "I've been returning to a quote by Dumbledore that I want to share. I hope it brings some semblance of comfort, as we all try to figure out how the world hasn't stopped even though it has a gaping six-five, 135-pound hole in it. 'Happiness can be found in even the darkest of times, if one only remembers to turn on the light.'"

Sarah will tell you now that Dumbledore's advice didn't always work. There are some days when the light doesn't turn on. But in the moment, Dumbledore comforted everyone.

Elizabeth began by describing how theirs had not been the stereotypical older brother–younger sister relationship because Max didn't pick on her. She described a conversation in which Max had confided in her about his concern for a friend who had lost a job and a relationship.

"I wish Max had used the same sense of trust with a friend or family member to reach out about what was going on in his life, just as he had helped his friend," she said. "When I asked Max what advice he had given his friend, he said that he told him to just keep going, that it would get better in time, and that he was strong enough to get through it all."

She applied that same advice to the four of us.

"There's a famous Winston Churchill quote that says, 'When you're going through hell, keep going,'" Elizabeth said. "Right now we are going through hell, and we probably will be for a long time to come. But just as Mr. Churchill said, and just as Max advised his friend just over a year ago, we just have to keep going."

When it was my turn, I looked out at all the people and resolved myself to try not to focus on anyone. If I did, I would collapse into a puddle. I read the room and decided I needed to set the tone.

"I think you'll find the first forty-five minutes of this are rough," I said. "But then I will settle into a rhythm."

I smiled, just to make sure they got the joke. And they laughed, which relaxed us all.

"Max's death has shone a light on the innate goodness in people," I began, "a quality that I am sure I didn't appreciate until now.

"I think of that as a gift from our son. I have to say, Max, that on the whole, I would have preferred a dozen golf balls."

(Within days after the service, I received four dozen golf balls from friends who attended or read my remarks.)

I spoke of who Max was, much of which served as the foundation for the previous chapters. I explained the erratic nature of his last hours, which we pieced together after his disappearance. I explained how we tried to parent Max, and I explained how it had blown up in our faces.

Charlie Chaplin was once asked how to improve the classic visual joke of a man and a banana peel. His solution: the man walks down the street. There's a shot of a banana peel on the street ahead. Show the man, oblivious to the danger. Show the peel. Show the man approaching. Peel. Man. Peel.

At the last second, as the audience is prepped and poised to see the pratfall, the man sees the peel and steps around it. Self-satisfaction spreads across his face. Crisis averted. Maybe even a jaunty look. The man takes one step—and goes right down an open manhole.

I always thought, if we can get Max through the hell of high school, he will go to college, find himself, find his people and he will blossom. Max began to find himself. He found his people.

And he stepped right into a manhole.

As he told a counselor at RIT that he had no intent to hurt himself or others, he told a couple of online friends that he wanted to disappear. We noticed that he had gone underground, but this was a matter of degrees. Max disliked talking on the phone. We assumed it was just the normal pressures of college.

We were wrong.

There is circumstantial evidence to indicate that Max intended to take his own life. The Rochester police tell us they will not connect the dots. But you don't have to be a pointillist to see a larger picture. We live at a time when suicide is recognized as a result of mental illness, when the stigma has been removed. Even if it weren't, we have never been ashamed of Max, and we aren't going to start now.

And yet. And yet.

Suicide can be an impulsive act; or, as my fellow Mobilian Jimmy Buffett sang about tattoos, a permanent solution to a temporary problem. Really, what difference does it make? Accidental or intentional, he's gone. Either path leads to the result that we don't have him anymore.

We have learned over the last month that hindsight is not 20/20. It is, in fact, a hall of mirrors, distorting memory, assigning motive and meaning where it may not belong.

It is tempting to think of this as a version of *It's a Wonderful Life* with the last reel missing. Clarence didn't save Max, who, as a result, didn't realize the impact his life had on all of us.

In the end, we may never know what happened. All we do know is that Max tried to leave the room—quietly.

Meg and I both felt strongly that we didn't want to scramble about after Max's death, cleaning up details that would make others uneasy. Sanitizing Max's death felt tawdry to me, as if it would somehow misrepresent him, cheapen what he had endured, and to what end? To make our family look better? I can't tell you how little I cared about how the four of us looked to people outside the house. Sanitizing Max's death sure wouldn't make us feel better. The bottom line was we didn't have Max. Someone else could dress up why we didn't have him. We weren't going to do it.

About ten days later, we received a note from David Bauer, who had been an executive editor of *Sports Illustrated* when I worked there more than a decade earlier. I think I had seen him once since I left for ESPN in 2002. "When I walked into the memorial service, I did not know Max at all," David said. "When I walked out, I did, and I missed him and I loved him. I'm deeply sad that that's the way I had to meet Max, but I'm grateful to know him. How you two, and your daughters, made that happen is something extraordinary."

Hearing that from David, or anyone, really, made us feel that the memorial service had achieved what we hoped it would. Another good friend dropped a note calling the memorial service "the most beautiful sad affair." Yes.

Having said that, I will tell you that mourning a death by mental illness brings a unique burden. It would seem to me that with other illnesses, we survivors limit our liability to how quickly we recognized the symptoms in our loved ones, how quickly we convinced them to seek treatment. Otherwise, we blame the disease. We're not quite there as a society with mental illness. We're closer, but we still tend to blame the victim, or ourselves, for the victim's inability to "snap out of it." I concluded fairly quickly that I could live with blaming mental illness, but I did daydream about how our grief might differ had Max died from a cause other than mental illness—an auto accident, gun violence, or any of the myriad sudden, heartbreaking demises that befall the eighteen-to-twenty-four age cohort. Would it be less painful to us?

That is a useless notion. The more I thought about it over the ensuing months, the more I understood that all unexpected deaths deliver a unique burden. Some are just heavier than others.

After the service, we flung open the doors to our country club—that's a metaphor; it was still frightfully raw on that early spring weekend. But we invited everyone who came to the service, and we plied all those who came with food and drink, the equivalent of a fourth Bar/Bat Mitzvah celebration in our three-child family. Meg and I treasured our wedding, and the Bar/Bat Mitzvahs of our children, as celebrations with the people in our lives who meant the most to us. Max's memorial service felt like the photo negative of those parties. So many people showed up for us, and the needle on the day remained pointed at awful.

The last thing I wanted to do was work the rooms of a reception filled with hundreds of people, even if the hundreds of people were my family and friends, there to support us. I decided they could entertain one another, and I quickly retreated to the back of the reception, never straying far from the eight college buddies who had traveled to Connecticut to be by my side. They came from California and Texas, Oklahoma and New York. They knew no one else in the room. I see my college friends rarely, so I established them as my safe harbor. There is something about the relationships we build in college that endures for a lifetime. Besides, the last thing I wanted to do was eat or drink. Over three hours I had one chicken tender and one cocktail. I didn't feel compelled to talk to my extended family or my Fairfield friends. The willingness of my Stanford buddies to fly across the country to demonstrate their support meant so, so much. At the reception, and again at our house that night, I stayed near the friends I had made when I was Max's age.

All of which leads to Elizabeth's news. We closed the reception down around 4 p.m. and returned to our house, family, our college friends, and other out-of-towners in tow. Within the hour, Elizabeth found me and said, "Can I talk to you for a minute?" She wheeled around and led me upstairs, to my room. I closed the door, and she said, "I didn't get into Michigan." She was dispirited, defeated. On the edge of sobbing, she said, "If I can't get into Michigan, I'm not going to get into Stanford." I clearly had forgotten—again—what it feels like to be a high school senior. She had reminded me only hours earlier, when she got what may have been the biggest laugh among our three eulogies.

"Over this past Christmas break, one night at dinner," Elizabeth said, "my mom brought up something regarding college applications that really annoyed and upset me. The fight ended with me storming away from the table crying, offended by the advice that [my parents] were trying to give me. Later that night, Max said to my mom, 'I know I'm not great at social skills, but you two really screwed that one up.'"

So much for thinking that a sister returning home from her brother's memorial service might have received some perspective about an admissions decision. There we were, winding up one of the days on the medal stand for the Worst Maisel Day Ever, in a house teeming with people, bracing ourselves for yet more heartbreak that the 1-in-20 odds would deliver.

Five years earlier, I held the naive belief that Sarah would gain admission to Stanford, and I never wavered in that belief. In the interim, I had written a story about the difficulty of admissions for *Stanford Magazine* that cured me of my naivete. I worried that Elizabeth's improvement in her standardized test scores would be seen as the fruit of an educated, wealthy household instead of the leading indicator that she had worked really hard. I worried that, as I reported the magazine piece, I had a conversation with the assistant dean of admissions in which I said that Elizabeth had the most common sense of anyone I knew but not the ravenous intellectual curiosity of her sister, and that the dean would hold that against her. That's what is known as benign arrogance—as if, in a sea of forty-two thousand applications, the dean would have (a) been assigned Elizabeth's application, (b) recognized her name, and (c) recalled the conversation.

I relayed none of that to Elizabeth. I tried to calm her. What I failed to realize is that none of us—Meg, Sarah, or I—ever informed Elizabeth of the distinct probability that she would be hearing from Stanford in about an hour. She still thought she would hear the following Tuesday.

By a couple of minutes after 6 p.m., the house already had filled to the point that you had to raise your voice to be heard. I remember standing in our front hall, looking in at Meg and some of my extended family arrayed around our dining room table. Sarah coaxed Elizabeth upstairs and suggested she check her email, and Elizabeth assured her that she wouldn't hear from Stanford for another few days. Sarah told her that she had just looked at the university website and that the decisions had been released. They sat on the edge of Elizabeth's bed. The Wi-Fi signal doesn't travel well to that part of the house in normal circumstances; now the house was filled with people and phones. Elizabeth had to refresh a couple of times, tough to do when your hands are shaking.

In a matter of seconds that only felt like hours, the email arrived. Elizabeth clicked on it. All she and Sarah saw was the word, "Congratulations!"

Sarah leapt in the air and shrieked, and they bolted downstairs, hitting each stair with all their weight, not unlike Max every time he emerged from his room, except that the girls were yelling and crying. Meg and I locked eyes, hers and mine brimming with tears.

The news cut through the layer of sadness that pressed down upon our home. To see Elizabeth beam with pride and happiness and relief, to see her celebrated by a house full of family and friends, well, there just couldn't have been a sweeter tonic. The juxtaposition of that happiness against the backdrop of a memorial service for our son and her brother was just one more piece of this-can't-be-happening. Meg called Stanford's acceptance Max's gift to Elizabeth. That is an easy connection to make, and at the time I refused to make it. It seemed too pat. It didn't make me feel better about Max's death or Elizabeth's success. I appreciate the sentiment more today.

Later that night, we gathered the dozen Stanford grads in the house, ranging from 1977 to 2014, my generation and Sarah's classmates, to take a photo with Elizabeth Maisel, class of 2019. Everyone is smiling, Elizabeth wearing the biggest smile of all. I am wearing one of Max's flannel shirts. It remains one of my favorite photographs of my life.

Elizabeth (*fourth of five in the front*) with the Stanford grads a short time after she heard she had been accepted.
Photo courtesy of the Maisel Family

But morning dawned, and with it the reality that everyone who cared for us and had rushed to our side now had to return to reality, the last place I wanted to be. Once they were gone, we would be left with the yawning chasm where Max once had been. A few days earlier, when Genevieve Reilly, the local reporter, had come to the house, Meg said something to her that became the "kicker"—the end of the story.

"Both of us, we're very aware that Chapter Two of the hard part starts after Friday," Meg said.

I hadn't slept much on that Friday night, so my emotions already rode a little closer to the surface. I got choked up hugging Max's cousins goodbye. Max had been one of them. I understood how they felt about him and how they felt about not having him. By the time

I hugged my brother Elliot, the emotional center and all-but-titular head of our extended family since the death of our father seven-plus years before, tears streamed down my face. I didn't want to lose my brother's presence.

A few days later, Elliot called and told me about a golf match he and his oldest son had played against two friends, and the conversation made me so sad. It wasn't the golf that stung. My brother and I have discussed our golf games with one another in excruciating detail for years. It was my brother spending time with his son, an experience I could no longer parallel. Not to mention, I understood that I would be witnessing or hearing about their days together for a long, long time. That may have been one of my first realizations that the pain bearing down on me wouldn't go away with a couple of Motrins and a good night of sleep.

Every Thanksgiving weekend, Elliot and I take on his two sons in an annual generational grudge golf match. It has become a signature event of my favorite holiday. We compete and laugh and taunt, hole after hole, year after year. Elliot's sons have both married since Max died, and they are now parents of babies. I love Elliot's sons dearly. And even now, as I have become accustomed to carrying my grief, as I have learned to maneuver around the shoals of reminders of loss that occasionally and regularly appear, the match stings just a little. It always will.

Chapter Six

A Ball Under Water

Sarah combines a voracious intellect with high emotional sensitivity. In short, she plays emotional chess while I, the older, more mature of us, am drawing up a tic-tac-toe grid. When Max disappeared, Sarah, eight months a college graduate, flew east from the Bay Area to join us in Rochester. She wanted to come on that first day, Tuesday, but we told her to wait until we could get up there and eyeball everything. That gave her time to get her life in order before she came east. It also gave her time to read about sisters who lose a brother and parents who lose a son. Shortly after she landed, she cornered me and Meg to ask us a question.

"Are you two getting divorced?" Sarah blurted. "I read that half of parents who lose children get divorced."

My memory is of wanting to dismiss her question out of hand to reassure her without insulting the intelligence it took to ask in the first place. The Flying Wallendas come to mind.

"No, sweetie," I said, looking from Meg to Sarah. "That's not going to happen."

I'd like to think I added, "One disaster at a time," although I don't think I'm that quick, especially on as little sleep as I had gotten while standing in the debris field where my life had been seventy-two hours earlier. Meg and I already had promised each other that we would not allow losing Max to tear apart the life we had built. We had come too far, built too strong a foundation, made too many compromises not to repair this damage.

Meg and I met in New York City in the fall of 1982. She went to Cornell with an old friend of mine named Dean. When all three of us landed in Manhattan after college, I moved in with Dean, and Meg began stopping by the apartment. Meg and I started out playing it cool. We both understood our relationship, or fling, or whatever it was we were doing, would never go anywhere. Meg grew up Catholic and had never lived outside of New York State. I grew up Jewish and crossed off the days until I could return to the South. In that sense, we found in each other a secure parking space. We could have fun together without worrying that it would ever turn serious.

Thus began what we always have called a "whirlwind six-year courtship." It took us six years to successfully leap over the hurdles presented by our traditions and our upbringings, by our families and our Rand McNallys. Meg looked into Judaism, even took a conversion class, before deciding she couldn't do it. But she agreed to raise our children in the Jewish faith. I agreed that our long-range plan would be to live not in Mobile as I always had envisioned, but in the Northeast. She won geography, and I won religion, and when I look back at the bargaining table with the perspective of nearly four decades, some of me wonders why I made such a fuss. I see the hurt each of us experienced in what we surrendered to make our partnership work.

I can live with what I gave up. As I explain to southerners with a shrug, "My children talk funny." But, for example, I wonder still what I actually gained with my adamancy that we not celebrate Christmas in our house. Instead, we traveled to Syracuse every year and celebrated it at my in-laws' house. Those four or five nights at the Residence Inn in Syracuse ranked among the best nights of Max's year. At home, we would not allow Cece, our yellow lab, to sleep on a people bed. In our hotel suite, Meg and I took one bedroom, the girls another, and Max got to sprawl with Cece on the sofa bed. That made Max (and Cece) very happy.

I suppose what Meg and I gained by working out the conditions of our life together is that we created ourselves as a unit. It helped that we became best friends. We like being physically active. We think alike politically. We agree that I have a great sense of humor (sorry, I have a Jewish mother, so I grew up being told how wonderful I am). We are both pleasers, by personality and birth order. She is the sixth of eight, I am the third of three. That last trait may have been the most important of our marriage. We often defer to each other's wishes, sometimes with a teasing comment that we used on the kids, too: "You do you."

The philosophy behind that comment came to the fore in that first week after Max disappeared. Meg and I decided that we would not judge each other's grief. I am embarrassed to say I had never come across the work of David Kessler, one of the foremost experts on grief, until I began to put this book together. It turns out that Meg and I had stumbled onto the key to staying married.

"I do not believe a child's loss is what causes a divorce," Kessler told Brené Brown in a March 2020 episode of her podcast, *Unlocking*

Us. "I believe judgment of each other's grief causes divorce. What happens is we all grieve differently. We all believe if we lose our child we are going to grieve exactly alike. Then if we don't grieve exactly alike, we begin to make up stories that aren't true."

Man, did Meg and I grieve differently. As open as I profess to be about my grieving, I still practiced pain avoidance. I didn't go to great effort to find out what happened. That may have been a luxury I enjoyed because Meg turned over every rock between RIT and Lake Ontario. She wanted to know everything. For nearly three years, she confronted Max's death with persistence. She needed to know everything she could discover about what happened and why.

I didn't have the stomach for that. I still don't. Whatever we found out wasn't going to bring Max back to life. It was just going to make me dwell on the loss. Max's death became the proverbial hot stove in our lives. A lot of days, I would tease Meg by asking her, "Burn your hand?"

But I understood she had to do it. She needed markers. She needed totems. She needed white lines to drive between after our lives careened out of control. We put up a headstone and buried some of Max's ashes at our family plot in Fairfield. Meg visited two or three days a week for a long time. I started out going a couple of times of month and didn't even maintain that pace.

Meg not only joined a suicide survivor support group; she became friends with the facilitator. I went once. My therapist, Debra, is not a grief counselor per se. But she is a Maisel counselor. She knew me, knew Meg, knew how we thought and how to help us. I leaned on her, and I found great relief from awakening before dawn and pouring my thoughts, my pain, my grief into my laptop.

Meg bought two shelves of books about grief, mental health, and suicide. I gained little from the ones that I picked up, an exception being *Riding with the Blue Moth*, the book that Bill Hancock, the executive director of the College Football Playoff, wrote after the death of his son Will in a plane crash in 2001. Bill always brings an understanding ear to our conversations. We speak the shorthand of the Club No One Wants to Join, a language unfamiliar to many. The fact is, most people didn't know what to say or didn't know that they didn't know what to say and spoke anyway.

When friends and acquaintances said something clumsy to us, or didn't support us well, or at all, I looked at them and recognized myself for the first fifty-five years of my life. Meg had no tolerance. She felt great pain, and the last thing she wanted to do was spend time with someone who didn't feel emotionally safe to her, no matter how long their previous relationship.

Meg and I listened to each other. We dried one another's tears. We counseled each other when asked. Yet we attended grief counseling separately, unless we had an issue that we couldn't resolve or that affected one of the girls. That brings to mind something else that Kessler told Brown.

"Two people with an empty tank cannot fill each other up," Kessler said. "Yet that is what we try to do."

Somehow, we understood to loosen the reins on one another. The impetus to do so may have come from my former *SI* colleague Frank Deford's 1983 memoir, *Alex: The Life of a Child*, about his daughter, who had died three years earlier of cystic fibrosis at the age of eight. Deford published the book shortly after Meg and I started dating; it may have been the first book I recommended to her. Its power remained with us more than three decades later. After Max went missing, Meg and I remembered the agreement that Frank and his wife, Carol, had struck—they would not cry at the same time. We adopted that rule and agreed that we would not judge one another.

That decision to loosen the reins kept our amputated lives intact. In 2019 we celebrated our thirtieth wedding anniversary. Our marriage is stronger for having survived Max's death. It is a happy marriage, as happy as any part of our lives can be having lost a son. We aren't getting a divorce anytime soon.

In the days after the memorial service, when everyone who loved us returned to their own lives and we remained behind, out of adrenalin and tethered to our loss and pain, I suffered some low moments. Take this passage that I wrote in my laptop that week:

I spent most of the day wondering if I would be this depressed forever. It. Is. Awful. There are so many facets of the awfulness.

The how unhappy he was awful.

The how much pain he must have been in awful.

The we didn't know awful.

The built-in guilt that comes with the last one and the entirety of the woulda coulda shoulda awful. It. Does. No. Good. And yet it is difficult to resist. Meg focuses on so many things. I think about that last month, when I realized he had been in even less communication than normal, and I didn't reach out. I was wrapped in my own petty, stupid, they-are-so-embarrassing-now issues, and he had stayed behind his walls for his five weeks here. I didn't sound the alarm. I didn't grab him and shake him and say what is wrong? We can help! Two weeks ago, I think, and I don't remember if I wrote this or not, but I drove down the street, repeating louder and louder, "We would have done anything!" until I shouted it, and then my voice cracked, and I said it twice more in an emotional, exhausted rasp. We didn't know.

The we may never know awful. The questions he left.

The he was a good son and we took that for granted awful. That one hit me yesterday. Max was a good son. He did what we asked. He was utterly devoted to us.

The we no longer have him awful.

The we want our life back awful.

The emptiness awful. The pit in the stomach. Feeling like an amputee.

The energy it takes to re-enter the civilian world awful. People are living their lives, as we did, and have no idea what it takes to step into that, to think and focus on other subjects, to laugh, to move on. As much concern as they have expressed and continue to express for us, they move on. They get to move on. We remain behind. We carry the burden. They don't.

The day after I wrote that, I pulled into the parking lot of our neighborhood grocery (Another reason Meg and I get along: I like to shop for food. She does not.) and called my mother to wish her a Happy Passover. We talked about the seder, the ceremonial meal held on the first night of the eight-day holiday. We talked about the weather in Mobile. We talked about how Meg and I and the girls were holding up.

"I want you to know," she said, "that I think about Max every day." That sounds more simplistic than she meant it. She went on to describe how someone who is that integral a part of your life, like Max, like my dad, who had died in 2007, four weeks after their sixtieth anniversary, remains a constant presence. I started to choke up, which made me react, "Seriously? Again? I am going to keep falling apart?"

We chatted for a little longer. I hung up and just remained in my car for a minute. I immediately realized the idiocy of my reaction.

Of course, I am going to keep falling apart. I needed to keep falling apart. I just needed to understand that I would keep falling apart so that I wouldn't feel ambushed when it happened. That's when it began to dawn on me: Max's death isn't going away. Missing him isn't going away. His absence will be, as Mom said, my constant companion. Everywhere I go, his absence will go with me, stand beside me. Actually, I pictured his absence, my grief, my pain, on my shoulder. Not a shadow, just a presence.

This phrase came into my head: It just is. *Is* as a verb, not as a bridge to another verb. His absence just exists. It just is.

I repeated that sentence to myself as I walked across the parking lot into the grocery. Coming to that understanding calmed me. It just is. It will always be right here, on my shoulder. Get used to it. Learn to live with it. It's not scary. It's not dangerous. It's just . . . there. It just is.

That thought gave me the first peace I enjoyed since Max disappeared. This was my grief. A survivor learns to grieve, to acknowledge the loss, to understand that it is never going away. In a sense, the permanence of the loss replaces the person lost—a poor replacement, initially alienating and painful in its omnipresence, eventually a burden you become accustomed to carrying. I don't have Max anymore. I have his loss. Grieving is the vehicle for accepting that transformation. Eventually, every survivor makes the transformation. The question is, at what pace? Those who choose to stiff-arm the grief will find their arms get awfully tired after a while. The force of grief is inexorable, an inflated ball rising through water. It will emerge into open air, either when the griever desires or when the grief desires, which may not be at an opportune time.

Nor do our balls rise through the water at the same speed. Neither Meg nor the girls enjoyed the same "Eureka!" moment upon hearing my discovery. It just is? They looked at me like I had just announced the discovery of air. That deepened my understanding that each of us grieved on our own paths at our own pace. Meg needed to know everything she could know, good and bad, revelatory and painful, about how Max had gone into this irreversible slide. Me, I was in my fifty-sixth year of shying away from pain, from discomfort. I edged up to every bad feeling as if I were dipping my toe into an ice bath.

And yet I knew at some level that I had to experience the pain before I could shed it. I had to dip my toe, my foot, and the rest of me until I fully immersed myself, until my body and my spirit were completely accustomed to it. For me, Max's laptop became an emotionally fraught version of *Let's Make a Deal* (Max loved Wayne Brady, the host, from his improv work on *Whose Line Is It Anyway?*): In this file, beautiful examples of Max's photographic skill. In this file, Max's self-assessment from his OkCupid account. It is dated January 23, 2015, the day after his anime hero Monty Oum slipped into a coma.

I wish I could see in me the things my friends do. I wish I could see my own worth. But I can't. And I'm so buried in negativity and cynicism that I doubt I ever will.

Reading that may have been my lowest point. It was one thing for me to understand that he had died because of mental illness. Here was evidence that Max understood he was not well and couldn't find a way back to good mental health. I keep in mind that college is a time when people are transforming into adults, and the pressure of academics and relationships produces severe highs and severe lows. I am struck by his acknowledgment that others saw good traits in him. He was aware of that, and yet it couldn't sustain him.

Poor Max. Poor, poor Max.

He needed help, and he didn't get enough of that to sustain him, either. It just broke my heart. I love him. I loved him. I didn't always understand him. But all I wanted was for him to be happy, to find happiness. He couldn't get there. He wanted to get there, and he couldn't get there. God, the pain he must have been in. The pain he must have been in that all he wanted to do was stop it. That ending his life looked to him to be the best alternative. Walking onto that pier in that weather seemed like a better alternative. Years passed before I looked up the weather in Rochester that night: 10 degrees and "ice fog." Walking onto that pier in that weather with little sleep and little food in his system.

I used to politely detour around sadness. Didn't want to write about it, didn't want to read features about it, definitely didn't want to read sad novels or watch sad films. I didn't want the burden. Now I had a burden all my own. It belonged to me and always would. I had to get on living with it.

Meg dug up a cardboard Father's Day "tie" that Max had made for me in first or second grade. She hung it in my closet. On the back of the tie, in the illegible, phonetic scrawl of a child learning to write, Max provided a list of Father's Day gifts, tasks he would perform and outings we would take. I am reasonably certain that when Meg handed it to me, it was the second time I ever thought about it. The tie is painful for me, and yet I keep it hanging in my closet. I want to be reminded that I never followed up on actually receiving any of Max's proposed gifts. He would put things away. He would wash my car. He would make his bed. He would bring me breakfast in bed. We would play games one night a week. We would go golfing. And so on. It's so sweet, and it hurts every time I look at it.

I want to be reminded that I didn't make time for him while I was off making a career. I also want to be reminded of a more innocent time, of Max the sweet boy who became the sweet young man over-whelmed by conditions over which he could exert little control. The rigidity of his life, the disciplines he forced on himself and the rest of us, must have been a method of controlling the chaos in his mind.

More from the laptop: Meg found a cache of photos from You-macon, the anime convention that Max attended in Detroit. The photos portray Max with his online friends, including Shauna, his girlfriend. The pics are so normal, friends standing together smil-ing, and yet they make me profoundly sad. We had met the carful of kids who traveled with Max from RIT. But we don't know them well, and whatever relationship we had with them didn't extend be-yond Max's life. The others in the photos? Besides Shauna, we have no idea who they are. We see them in rare photos of a smiling Max, or at least a Max without the driver's-license-photo face that he typ-ically adopted.

With both Sarah and Elizabeth, we met their friends during freshman year and watched them mature into adults together. Each of the girls has remained close with her freshmen crew. We attended a wedding of one of Sarah's friends. We hosted a bunch of Eliza-beth's for a beach weekend. That is the way life is supposed to work. In Max's case, I felt doubly cheated. We don't have Max. Because he kept to himself, because he kept so much inside, we didn't have his friends. We didn't have them to commiserate with. After Max dis-appeared, we heard from a few of those friends, describing a side of him that we didn't know.

"That very particular laugh of his, where each 'hah' built upon the last," a friend named Kate wrote us, "and the way he would usu-ally follow up with 'Oh, that's good' or 'I actually really like that' or something to make it just more personal. I especially remember it in the context of him laughing at my jokes. As has been said of him numerous times, he had a very special way to make sure you knew he was listening and that he cared about every word he heard you say."

A transgender friend told us about the unconditional support Max provided them, which I found fascinating. As uncomfortable as Max could be around people, and as emotionally immature as he was, his tolerance and empathy made Meg and me confident that he would find his way. On Thanksgiving weekend his sophomore year, 2013, various Maisels lounged around, doing what we do every Thanksgiving—eating and chitchatting. As you may have guessed by now, Max didn't do chitchat. He was in the room physically and, we assumed, on his iPad in every other way.

Max's cousin Michelle, thirteen years his senior, began describing how a woman she had gone to high school with had decided not to get married until gay marriage was legalized.

"Why?" my sister Kathy asked. "She isn't gay, right?"

She's not. But before Michelle could answer, Max, without looking up from his iPad, piped up.

"Uh, maybe she just values basic human rights."

I'm pretty sure the whole room turned and looked at him.

What none of us knew at that moment is that another cousin in the room, Rebecca, was on the cusp of coming out. After Max died, Rebecca wrote us an email reminding us of this story.

"Of course I was getting tense, and perked up, because that's an important issue to me," Rebecca said. "I'll never forget it. It's small, but it made me smile."

Shortly after Max disappeared, one friend from the neighborhood, Gordon Crean, wrote us a beautiful letter from Geneva, where he was studying abroad. Gordon described their soaring flights of imagination together during elementary school and the connection they maintained in middle school, when he found Max to be "incredibly funny and quick-witted, sensitive, always willing to listen and offer advice. He was amazingly genuine." Gordon described his regret that they had grown apart in high school and how he hoped his letter "reflected a little bit of the light left behind by Max."

Gordon is now a psychologist, working on his PhD and practicing in Massachusetts. I have resisted the urge to romanticize Max or his life. I loved him. I still love him. But I like to remember people as they were. That said, I like to think Max will play a role in Gordon's ability to help people who need help, that Max will inspire Gordon as he pursues his life's work. I ask questions for a living. That's one question I don't want to ask Gordon. I like my preferred answer a little too much.

A couple of years after Max died, Meg and I took the train into New York to see a Sunday matinee on Broadway. As we walked through Grand Central Station to catch the ride home, I felt a tap on my right shoulder. It was Seb, the son of our neighbors, Max's age, an affable "normal" kid who grew up alongside Max, if not with him. They were friendly, not friends. Max, from his space somewhere on the spectrum, had little in common with Seb besides a street address. Seb loved sports as a boy, went to a big-time sports university, and graduated into a career in the business of sports. He is climbing the career ladder. Seb has grown into a young man with a business haircut. The hair in his eye has been shorn and replaced by a gleam. He is hungry and ambitious and well mannered and, on this night in Grand Central, excited to see us.

Seeing Seb in Grand Central, returning home after working on a Sunday, triggered within me a depth of pain and longing. I held it together long enough to chitchat with him, even as seeing him ripped apart my insides. He is on his way. Max is receding in history, remaining where he left us.

In the first few months, I did find a lot of relief on the golf course, if for no other reason than I had four hours to concentrate on something else. A couple of weeks after the memorial service, on the first day our golf course opened for the season, a gray, raw, 42-degree day, my friend Tom Reilly and I showed up at the first tee at midmorning. We were the only two people on the course that day. I needed to be there. Tom happily accommodated me. Even as I took refuge on the course, I would find myself walking down the fairway, talking to Max, talking to myself, trying to reassure both of us. I would apologize to Max for not fully understanding his despair. I would give myself permission to be out there in the first place.

The following week, after a lot of discussion, I decided to travel with a group of sixteen friends that Tom put together to play golf in the Bay Area over a long weekend. Meg swallowed her pain and agreed to my going. She knew it would make me feel better, which it did, right up until Friday evening. My golf buddies and I sat in the bar at the Olympic Club, having completed thirty-six holes, when a detective from Rochester called. Cell phone calls are not allowed inside the club. I got up and walked out of the bar and went into the men's locker room. The scene is indelibly pressed upon my brain because that's where I learned that a fisherman in Lake Ontario came across a body floating a quarter mile off shore. The police would not confirm that it was Max until the coroner examined him. But the detective described a tall, thin male wearing a flannel shirt.

I was scheduled to come home Sunday, and I chose not to come home before then. There was nothing for us to do until the coroner made an identification (we had already sent Max's dental records to the Rochester police). The unselfish thing to do would have been for me to say goodbye, return to the hotel, pack, and take the red-eye home, thirty-six hours early. I did not, in part because Sarah was in San Francisco, and I wanted to see her after we got this news. But I still don't feel good about that decision. I got home Sunday, and at the first of the week, Meg returned to Rochester. She answered the coroner's questions. She waited as the coroner released the body to the funeral home. She picked up Max's ashes and drove seven hours home. Meg felt she needed to do it. I was all too happy to cede those duties to her. I don't know if I would have been strong enough to handle it. Meg had a support system that held her upright through the darkest times: her sister Maureen, who rarely left her side in Rochester, and her best friend from college, Anne Pride, who listened and listened and listened.

Around this time, my therapist, Debra, gave me a quote that she thought applied to us: "All that love could do was done." That sentiment helped immensely. What errors we committed, we did so with the best of intentions, or out of fear, or ignorance, those being the impetus for most well-meaning errors.

So—the errors I committed. Let me fill in a little bit more about me and Max. At several junctures in his life, he ran up against bad luck, tough moments, inconsiderate people, and I didn't step in to try to fix it.

Since Max resolutely refused to participate in any exercise, during high school we forced him to work out with a trainer once or twice a week. Max had trouble sleeping. We believed that if he made his body tired, it might help him, not to mention that Meg and I also are great believers in staying fit. Max developed a bond with the trainer. We had him over for dinner a time or two. And then one day, the trainer ghosted Max. Ghosted us. Stopped taking our calls. When he finally responded to Meg, he told her he couldn't deal with

Max's negativity anymore. That reaction is fine if you are a peer ill equipped to deal with a trait you don't like. This trainer was a grown man. Sure, he ended what had been a profitable relationship with the Maisel family, but that's not what frosted me. You just don't treat a vulnerable teenager that way.

In Max's junior year of high school, he took a work/study class in which he would get an internship at a local business in a field that interested him. He had caught the photography bug by then. He saved his money and bought a camera—from Elizabeth, whose fascination with her Nikon lasted about a month.

Max's internship with a local studio lasted one day. The owner, whom Meg had asked to participate so that Max would have a place to land, called the teacher after Max's first day and withdrew. We never learned why. But Max came home from school devastated. I didn't know the owner, wouldn't have recognized the name, face, anything. A few years later, I played in a charity golf tournament. A photographer stood by the eighteenth green, taking shots of each foursome after the golfers finished their round. I gave the photographer a big smile and said thanks. I learned the following day that the photographer had been Max's Employer-for-a-Day. It's probably for the best that I didn't know.

In the years since Max died, I have tried mightily not to judge people and how they handled Max's death, how they did or didn't interact with my grief. That trainer and that photographer, well, I haven't yet figured out how to forgive them. I still see the trainer occasionally in a gym. I'm immaturely brusque with him when I speak to him at all. But I don't do confrontations well, which is why I didn't get in their faces in the first place. Watching a child suffer is one of the most difficult experiences a parent will endure. Every dad has to decide whether to climb into the parental helicopter and hover over his children. But I haven't forgiven myself for failing to advocate for Max. One justification I provided myself is that high school sucks for everyone. If Max could just get through it, he would find his people in college.

I'm sure that I made the same sort of mistakes with my daughters. But I don't perseverate over those decisions. My daughters are still here. I keep saying I have more regrets than I do guilt. I may be kidding myself. Sometimes I think regret may be nothing more than guilt in a bespoke suit.

Chapter Seven

First-Evers

I wouldn't wish the first year of grieving on anybody.

Yes, the good news is that life goes on. It's learning how to function in this new world, the one you don't want to be in, the one without your son, that is so hard. The memorial service ends. The condolences no longer fill the mailbox—maybe it's a generational thing, but the written notes struck a deeper chord than did the emails. (It goes without saying that we loved getting notes no matter their route.) The meals stop arriving. We had to feed ourselves. We had to leave the house. The friends, even the best ones, return to their own lives, the good ones where their nuclear family remains intact.

Nuclear family. Ha. In our family the nuclear device went off.

There is no sugarcoating in the world that can soothe the first year following the death of a child. Every circled date on the family calendar—reunion, holiday, birthday, and, the newest circle, the anniversary of the death itself—is anticipated, feared, endured, and survived. For the most part, I refused to look too far down the road.

I had enough to do to make it through the day at hand, not to mention that I didn't want to face the emotional burdens that awaited me. I grew up biting my fingernails. I didn't quit until my late thirties, and only then after I gave myself an infection so painful that I went to the emergency room at 3 a.m. Nearly twenty years later, I started biting them again. Better than smoking, I guess.

The year would have been filled with emotional transition without losing Max. Elizabeth would graduate and be off to college. Meg and I would be alone together for the first time in twenty-three years. Debra, our family therapist, warned Elizabeth that her parents would have been acting weirdly emotional whether Max had died or not. I didn't have a lot of concern about living with Meg in an empty nest. We needed each other. We liked each other.

I am reminded of the old joke about the clergy arguing when life begins. The priest says at the moment of conception. The minister says when the fetus is viable. The rabbi says when the kids leave the house and the dog dies. I always liked that joke until it happened to me. A few weeks after Elizabeth left, our sixteen-year-old yellow Labrador retriever died. I'm not a big believer in assigning human motivations to pets, but Meg and I firmly believe that Cece had been near death when Max disappeared and she understood that she needed to stay alive for our sake. Meg tells me that, as with my father, I clung to the notion that Cece felt fine long after evidence had piled up to the contrary. I look at pictures of her from her final weeks and don't know what I could have been thinking. Actually, I know exactly what I was thinking—I needed her. I may have said that I would never give another pet IVs, as we did to keep Calvin alive, but I did take Cece to the vet two or three times a week during her last six months to receive laser treatments on her spine. She did the best she could to be there for us.

As injured as the four of us were, we all tried to open our hearts to the good, to let ourselves be happy when life presented happiness. Meg and I celebrated the tick-tock moments of Elizabeth's high school graduation. We gathered with other parents for picture-taking before senior prom. We didn't have much to say, but we showed up. We mustered genuine smiles for the graduation itself, and the four of us celebrated with a nice dinner afterward. But the feel-good shelf life of Elizabeth's achievement didn't last through the week. Since Sarah had returned home from San Francisco for the graduation, we decided to bury a portion of Max's ashes in our temple cemetery that week, too. We invited no one beyond our rabbi, who conducted a short service and stood aside as we buried the small leather-covered box. The four of us took turns shoveling the dirt back into the hole, a Judaic custom for mourners that Meg and I always appreciated.

We had decided to divide Max's ashes among four sites: Fairfield, Rochester, the Mobile area, and Steamboat Springs. The next stop would be in Rochester, when Meg and I returned for the annual late-summer reunion of her family at her brother Sean's lake house. Returning to the scene of Max's death didn't alarm me. Maybe it should have. Had I stopped to consider the emotional consequences, I might have better prepared myself. I had not been to Rochester since the girls and I left at the end of the awful, godforsaken, frozen week Max disappeared. Meg had gone back a few times. Meg needed to be there. Meg needed to be at the waterfront while the scuba team did its work. Meg needed to be there to retrieve Max's ashes. Now she and I would return, a portion of his ashes in tow. We wanted to spread them in Lake Ontario.

The girls didn't prepare themselves for the emotional consequences of returning to Rochester. They flat-out decided not to go.

You might think the weight of that decision would have registered with their dad. They had always loved seeing their cousins at the reunion, and yet they couldn't stomach going back to Rochester just yet. I didn't judge their decisions. I never thought whether I should refuse to go, either. I just went. It's a reunion! I would enjoy whoever chose to come.

On our typical route from Connecticut, we approach Rochester from the east. However, to avoid traffic, I drove farther west on the New York State Thruway and came in from the south (I drove by myself; Meg had come up earlier). My new route took me right past the RIT campus. As soon as I saw the familiar exits and shopping areas, the pit that had lodged in my stomach for that entire week in February excavated itself anew. It didn't remain there the whole weekend, but it slapped me into reality. I had come back to the scene of the worst event of my life.

I went into the house and said hello to everyone, drank half a beer, and chitchatted. There are a lot of Murrays, four generations now, and the family has adapted reunion behaviors to minimize housework. When you arrive, you get a plastic cup with your name on it for the long weekend. You get a towel for the long weekend. Max always used a brown-and-white vertically striped towel. Sean very thoughtfully had draped it over a chair on the porch. Max was there.

Still, from where I sat, and I imagine from where every one of the Murrays sat that weekend, Max cast a slight pall over the events. Not that we do much beside eat, drink, and hang out by the pool. At any hour, there are people at the pool, in the pool, around the pool, on the porch, in the den, in the kitchen, going to Wegman's—the grocery chain that feeds upstate New York—or walking to Charlotte Park one mile away, the location of the pier where Max stepped onto the frozen lake.

Photos courtesy of the author

We didn't hesitate to go to the park. In fact, we did just the opposite. Meg and I and the girls purchased a bench through the city parks division to install there. We wanted to commemorate Max's life and deliver a gift to the Rochester area for the care and concern they afforded all of us after Max disappeared. It's your typical park bench—wooden slats, iron frame—except for the bronze plaque on the back of the top slat.

MAX SULLIVAN MAISEL
JANUARY 15, 1994—FEBRUARY 22, 2015
BELOVED SON, BROTHER, COUSIN, FRIEND
WE LOVE YOU. WE MISS YOU EVERY DAY

The city placed the bench in an ideal spot, approximately a hundred yards west of the entrance to the pier, on the boardwalk directly in front of the beach volleyball courts on the shore of Lake Ontario. The bench sits somewhat in the shade of a mature tree. It is a pacific place in temperate weather: a massive body of water, a beach, a horizon with a pier and a lighthouse at the end of it. Meg said it is pretty much directly on the longitude of where the fisherman found Max's body.

The first time that Meg and I visited the bench, we found an older couple sitting on it, each of them reading. We debated whether to ask them to allow us to sit there. Instead, we approached them and asked them to separate so we could see the plaque. I might have told them that the plaque was our Max, if I could have gotten the words out. We stood there for a couple of minutes. I drank it in, waiting until I turned away from the strangers to tear up.

On Saturday afternoon, we invited all the law enforcement personnel who had searched for Max, from both the Rochester police and the Monroe County sheriff's departments, to the house for a barbecue. We felt an emotional bond with them. They had poured heart and soul into the search for Max. They might have worked so hard because Meg came down there every afternoon and thanked them. We never blamed them or castigated them for not finding Max. We felt only gratitude. We still couldn't believe that they had gone into near-freezing water day after day to look for him. We learned that summer that the leader of the Rochester police scuba team and his wife made a donation to the National Association of Mental Illness chapter in Rochester in Max's honor. Six years later, my heart swells just thinking of it.

That night, Meg and I stole out to the dock at the house to deposit Max's ashes in the lake several feet below. We wanted to do so ourselves, quietly, without the rest of the family. We didn't want anything ceremonial. We had no interest in a reprise of the memorial service. I'm not sure to this day how many members of the family realized that we did this.

In case you are wondering, the ash of a cremated body is not gray, like you see in a fireplace. It is kind of a muted rust, and there are flecks of white. That would be bone.

The wind had been steady all day, so we got on our knees at the edge of the dock. We each took handfuls of ash, held them below the dock, out of the wind, and let him slip through our fingers, an easy, if not quite accurate, metaphor for what happened to our boy. Here's another metaphor—we didn't execute this very well, either. That ash is very fine, and we kept letting it go before our hands dipped below the dock's edge. And did I mention there was a slight hole in the plastic bag?

Suffice it to say that when we got up from our knees, there was a little bit of Max everywhere. It was actually kind of comical— Max on the dock, on my navy-blue shorts, on Meg's pants, and I'm pretty sure every other surface within the wind's reach. If my laughing about that offends your sensibilities, well, we'll have to agree to disagree. We weren't being disrespectful. We were being inept. Big difference.

When we returned inside the house, no one noticed, or if they did, they had the grace not to say anything.

The next morning, before I got into the car for my drive home, I slipped quietly outside the house and returned to the bench myself. I did that by design. I wanted to soak in the scene, cement it in my mind for the fall and winter to come, feel Max's presence as best I could. By 10:30 a.m., the sky already had turned a brilliant robin's-egg blue. Low clouds settled to the west. The park already had a vibrant pulse. Big speakers played DJ-mix '80s music. I distinctly remember a mash-up of "Billie Jean," by Michael Jackson, and "Don't Stop Believin'," by Journey.

The bench stood empty, which surprised me. I took photos of it: the view from behind the bench, the bench with the park behind it. And I sat. I took a selfie of me and the plaque. I sat and dismantled my defenses, gazed at the light at the end of the pier and thought of Max. Whatever moment of peace that I had hoped to find, I found, and with great reluctance I stood and walked back to the house for the seven-hour drive to Fairfield that awaited me.

I walked slowly. I had been walking much more slowly and contemplatively than I did before Max died. I don't know if it was the fog of grief, or preoccupation, or just that I decided not to be in such a damn hurry anymore.

Later that year, our friend Bob Sussman bought and dedicated a bench to Max that sits in our neighborhood park in Fairfield. We received no lovelier gesture. The bench faces the toddler playground. We had it placed there for parents keeping a watchful eye. That seemed appropriate.

On Thanksgiving weekend, when the four of us gathered in Mobile with my side of the family, we took a portion of Max's ashes to the beach on Dauphin Island, a sliver of sand forty-five minutes south of Mobile. Max spent every July 4th week of the first ten years of his life on that island. My family's home there had been damaged by Hurricane Ivan in 2004 and destroyed by Hurricane Katrina the following summer. We didn't rebuild. The two storms had eroded our lot to about one-quarter of its original size. We didn't need a memo from the Environmental Protection Agency to understand what that meant. My family eventually sold what remained of the lot. Meg and I hadn't set foot on the island in more than a decade.

Max, age two and a half, dancing through bubbles at Dauphin Island
Photo courtesy of the Maisel Family

Four-year-old Max at Dauphin Island
Photo courtesy of the Maisel Family

As we stood at another shoreline with Max's ashes, I looked eastward down the beach. My father had loved that beach as he loved few other places on earth. Dad went to the beach house at every opportunity. He loved spoiling his grandchildren there. During the week every summer that my brother, sister, and I congregated there with our parents and our children, every afternoon Dad would make the coldest, thickest milkshakes you could suck through a straw. My memory is milkshakes were for grandchildren only. The ritual made such an impact on our kids that Elizabeth wrote a high school English paper about being four years old and "helping" her grandfather. Max may have subsisted on only a few foods, but he liked ice cream, and he loved his Papaw's milkshakes.

As I stood there on the beach, not quite far enough back from the gulf waters rolling onto shore, the memories flooded back. I thought about how I had been standing there looking at the gentle curve of that coastline for fifty years. My dad was gone, and now my son was gone, but recognizing that view of the beach helped stitch up the wound created by loss.

End-of-the-year holidays trigger depression for a lot of people who aren't mourning a child or brother. As Hanukkah and Christmas approached, the four of us reentered the cocoon we had built around ourselves in the weeks after Max disappeared. We had stopped going to Syracuse for Christmas the past few years, instigating a new tradition of going to a local steakhouse for Christmas Eve dinner. Max may have entered most restaurants with an air of trepidation, but he had sure footing in a steakhouse. He knew he would get a good piece of red meat, overcooked to his precise instruction. He knew he would get French fries. He knew he would eat baskets of bread.

Going back to the steakhouse would be just another example of highlighting the hole in our life—the reservation for four, not five. We went anyway. We had a nice, subdued, cholesterol-rich meal that must have shaved an hour or two off of my life, the kind of meal that caused me to awaken well before 5 a.m. on Christmas. I remained in bed for nearly an hour before I went downstairs to commune with Max, pull him down from the shelf where I placed him, like a keepsake, fully aware there are healthier ways to mourn.

I sat and watched the digital photo frame, once a lively piece of technology, scrolling through forty photos that he selected for his mother. After ten months of nonstop work, the frame had taken on Max's personality. Over five minutes it showed me the same four photos over and over. I saw only what it wanted me to see, which is so Max.

Meg ached for Max's touch. As a mom, she hugged him and touched him way more than I. My tactile memory of Max isn't a warm embrace. I have memories of carrying Max the baby and Max the toddler. My tactile memory of Max the young man is of awkward, tentative hugs, of trying to wade through an angular defense of limbs and joints, a geometric manifestation of the defense he erected for self-preservation. His defense took on many forms—sarcasm, cynicism, skepticism, isolation, maybe self-pity. I could never be sure if I misinterpreted his insecurities as self-pity. Maybe those defenses imprisoned him in the end.

Or maybe those defenses just crumbled.

I just missed him. One of the many compromises that Meg and I made in our partnership is that she wanted more than three children. As I said, she grew up the sixth of eight. But I was thirty-seven and Meg thirty-six when she had Elizabeth. I didn't want to be forty with a newborn, not to mention that Elizabeth took a greater physical toll on Meg in childbirth than Sarah or Max had. As I sat there on that Christmas morning, I realized again the price of convincing Meg to stop at three. I still thought we made the right decision. But I had become a lot less sure of it over the previous ten months.

Surviving the holidays on our family calendar was not the end but only the beginning of a fraught emotional period. Max, Sarah, and I all celebrated birthdays within a four-week span of the winter calendar. We approached the first-ever-birthdays-without-Max with trepidation.

Max's came exactly three weeks after Christmas, on January 15. He would have been twenty-two, even if it seemed ten years after his twenty-first. He still would have been home; classes at RIT wouldn't begin for another week. His birthday stirred so much sadness off the bottom of our memory jars. We had decided to spend the day doing Max things, a tradition that we have continued. We went to lunch at Super Duper Weenie, Max's favorite local burger joint. We went to a matinee to see the renewal of the Star Wars franchise, *The Force Awakens*, sitting in the dark, watching a sequel in a series in which we had long ago lost interest, staring at the screen in disbelief that Max was not there to see it.

The movie ended shortly after dark, and we headed around the corner to Timothy's, our local ice cream shop. Max went to Timothy's for years. He worked there the summer after his freshman year in college. The dead of winter is the very definition of downtime in an ice cream shop, especially in New England. Timothy was working by himself behind the counter. When we told him we had come to celebrate Max's birthday, he told us that the day also happened to be the thirty-third birthday of the store, a wonderful coincidence that Max didn't stick around to learn. Timothy refused to allow us to pay for the ice cream. He is a sweet, gentle soul, scarred by Max's death, too.

Exactly one week later, Meg awoke and said, "It's the first anniversary of the last day we saw him." That sentiment pretty much threw a cloud cover over our day. Meg had a catalog of the anniversaries in her head: last day we saw him, last day we spoke to him, last day we got a text from him. Right around then I combed through my texts with him, hoping to find a fresh trove of Max amid the daily bookkeeping ephemera of our lives, hoping to land upon some piece of previously unseen, or at least misunderstood, information. Max texted with the same economy of words as he spoke. And I recoil every time I read our last text exchange. I hadn't heard from him in a couple of weeks.

"You alive?" I wrote.

"In what sense?" Max replied.

"The breathing, not hearing from you sense," I said, continuing what I interpreted as our mutually shared dry wit.

"A little of both, in that case," he said.

The next text in our exchange is time-stamped Monday, February 23, at 7:50 p.m., eleven months earlier. I had just hung up the phone call from the sheriff, informing us that the bottom had dropped out of our lives.

"Call me," I sent.

The possible context of "In what sense?" remained lodged in my gut like a fist. I tried not to read too much into anything he did or said at the end of his life. I knew he had begun to lose his rationality, I knew I didn't really want to go there in the first place, and I knew that no matter what conclusion awaited me that it wouldn't bring him back.

My birthday arrived on January 26, reflecting my life in full as I turned fifty-six: happiness, love, sadness, all deeply felt. All I could think of was that for twenty-one years, Max had been my age minus thirty-four. Now he was my age minus thirty-five and counting. There would be other painful renderings of his absence. I wouldn't get a call from him. Max may not have liked to speak on the phone, but he never forgot a birthday. He may have been awkward in how he expressed it, but he remained caring and considerate.

We had begun to enlarge and remodel our kitchen. It had been stripped down to the insulation, with thick paper taped down to cover the wooden floor. The kitchen had needed to be replaced. The cabinet doors hung crookedly, as if their hinges had arthritis. The decor was tired, the appliances outdated. Our kitchen had lived a good life, and its time had come. When I wasn't standing in what remained of the kitchen that had served our needs for more than twenty years, I thought it still existed. I would think, "I need the scissors," only to walk in there and rediscover that the cabinets had left. Sarah and Elizabeth, living in California, thinking of us back home, saw us in a kitchen that no longer existed. And then I realized the kitchen in which Max grew up no longer existed. He will never see the new kitchen. Those thoughts walloped me, maybe because kitchens are where we live, maybe because food is love, maybe because the remodel became a very tangible symbol of how we had been forced to reconstruct our lives without Max. The kitchen looked like our lives for the past year, gutted and in need of restorative care. It reminded me of my hometown of Mobile after a hurricane has wreaked its destruction. You clean up the mess, and what you have left is a mass of scars and previously unavailable vistas.

For my birthday, Meg and I spent the night in New York and saw a Broadway revival of *Noises Off*, a British farce that, even if you were seeing it for the fourth time as I was, is endorphin-bomb funny. When we walked out of the theater on Forty-Third Street, I was hit by a wave of yearning for Max that nearly toppled me. Max and I had seen *Noises Off* in Hartford a few years earlier. I remember how hard he laughed, how much he enjoyed it. Now it had returned to Broadway, the major leagues compared to the triple-A production in Hartford, and he wasn't there to see it.

For the first anniversary of Max's death, Meg and I decided we wanted to be near the girls—Sarah lived in San Francisco, Elizabeth an hour south at Stanford—and far from the cold. We wanted as little sense memory of his disappearance as possible. We rented a small apartment in San Francisco for a month and headed west. We left early enough to celebrate Sarah's birthday in mid-February—another family milestone without Max—and settle in place for

February 22. On the day, we took a train down to Palo Alto, met Sarah, and the three of us went to "walk the Dish." High in the hills overlooking campus is an enormous radio antenna known as the Stanford Dish. The university installed it in 1961 for research. It has gained much wider use as the main attraction of a rolling 3.5-mile trail that provides breathtaking views of the campus, San Francisco Bay, and much of the peninsula.

When Elizabeth freed up, we grabbed her and went to dinner at a local burger joint. We decided to remember Max by having a Max meal. After stuffing ourselves with hamburgers (we all ordered buns—sorry, Max), we went for dessert at the Palo Alto Creamery, a modernized version of an old-fashioned soda fountain, complete with stools at the counter and tight booths. Max loved their milkshakes.

Long after we finished our shakes, we sat in our booth and tried to reconstruct the days after Max disappeared. We needed to be together on that anniversary. We needed to console one another that day. No one outside the four of us could understand with the same emotional specificity what we were going through. In that sense, Max's death bonded the four of us more tightly than we would have been otherwise.

Passing the one-year anniversary of Max's death made me understand—again—the permanence of the loss. The presence of his absence, and the absence of his presence, continued to be with me, sitting on my shoulder as I had pictured it the previous spring in the grocery store parking lot.

The last one-year anniversary arrived in the form of Jewish tradition. It is customary not to put up a tombstone for as long as eleven months after the death. At that time, family members participate in an "unveiling" ceremony. The mourners recite memorial prayers and reveal the tombstone for all to see. Meg and I own a two-person plot in our temple cemetery; with the congregation's permission, we had buried some of Max's ashes there and bought a tombstone large enough to hold the names of all three of us. The unveiling caught me at a low moment. The poet Edward Hirsch wrote a memorial ode to his son Gabriel in which he compared the work of grieving to carrying a bag of cement up an unending mountain. I knew that I had to continue to put one foot in front of the other. I knew that I had to continue to disgorge my feelings in a healthy way, either into my laptop or to a counselor, instead of pretending those feelings didn't exist.

As I emerged from the first year without Max, I began to see the perspective necessary to understand the permanence and nature of grief. Carrying that bag of cement every day exhausted me. But I began to understand that the pain wouldn't be acute every day. I began to see that when the pain grew acute, the next day, or maybe the day after that, wouldn't be as bad. I just had to lean into the pain, accept it, and wait for it to recede. I had learned enough to see that the grief would be endless, that it surged from the same fount as the love I had for Max. Making that connection between grief and love made it easier to withstand the pain of loss. I'm not a fan of advice worthy of greeting cards, but after Max died, one of our neighbors, whose husband had died suddenly and unexpectedly a few years earlier, repeated this to me: a griever is like a beachcomber at the shore. Sometimes the waves wash over your ankles. Sometimes they wash over your head. Either way, the waves recede.

The first year of mourning ended. The waves had washed over our heads quite a few times. We dried ourselves off and continued walking along the shore.

Chapter Eight

I Keep Trying to Catch His Eye

We made the decision to move to the Northeast in Max's infancy. Meg had made our future clear to me during her pregnancy with Max.

"I want to move back East," she said.

"I don't," I replied.

"You're not here!" she said. "You travel. I'm the one who lives in the house."

A quarter century later, I still don't have a response to that one. She had a point.

A few weeks after Max's birth, I heard through the sportswriting grapevine that *Newsday*, the Long Island daily, needed a college sportswriter. I had traveled enough with Tim Layden, who left that job for *Sports Illustrated*, to know that they wanted to cover the games I wanted to cover.

"I'm going to apply for a job at *Newsday*," I said to Meg.

"I don't want to leave Dallas *now*," she said.

"OK," I said. "Here's the phone number of the sports editor. You work it out with him."

Meg liked our life in Dallas. She had made friends in the Masters Swimming community. We had just begun to make the house we had bought not three years earlier into the home we wanted. And we had a toddler and a newborn. But you have to leave when the door is open. We moved at the end of June. Sarah was two, Max was five months, and I was AWOL. In an attempt to impress my bosses, I skipped the move to help cover the NBA Finals between the New York Knicks and the Houston Rockets. As we packed boxes, I sold my new editor on how easy it would be for me to hop from Dallas to Houston for games 6 and 7. I'd like to say that I considered how difficult the move would be for Meg. But that would be false. I wanted to prove myself. Not my finest moment in marriage.

Meg and I made a conscious decision not to live among the hard-charging, big-earning type As who commuted into Manhattan every day. We wanted to avoid getting caught up in the achievement arms race. We wanted to avoid living in a town we couldn't afford. For us to live in a tonier, wealthier suburb than the one where we put down roots would have been anywhere from a financial stretch to mortgage fraud. Besides, I had no desire to get any closer to New York City's gravitational pull. I didn't want my children to become pawns in some sort of next-gen competition between me and my neighbors. Meg and I had no desire to pay college-sized tuitions for private education. As products of public schools, we sent our children to public schools. We didn't demand that their report cards be filled with As. We expected their best efforts, and that was enough.

It was a reverse snobbery of sorts, the same chip I had always kept on the same shoulder. I am aware that I am considered to live among the swells. I graduated from a prominent university. I work among the media elite. My income allows us a comfortable life. But as I live on the inside looking out, I remain the southern Jew, the outsider looking in. Southerners of my generation with a conscience lived on the defensive. We lived with others expecting that we were prejudiced, not to mention the belief that because we spoke slowly, we thought slowly.

That's how I perceived the rest of the country looking at me. Growing up Jewish in the South in the 1960s and 1970s, you learned quickly that people made judgments about you before they knew you, that there existed clubs, fraternities, sororities, and friends who would never be available to you. If a journalist is by definition an observer instead of a participant, then you don't have to have a psychology degree to figure out how I landed in a metropolitan newsroom at age twenty-one.

It's also why I felt the way I did about living where and how we lived. We could achieve without bowing to social pressure. We could raise smart, healthy, well-adjusted children without suiting up for the rat race. We could win societal prizes playing the game our way, not their way. We didn't have to compete the way everyone else competed. We'd show them.

When Sarah gained admission to Stanford, our friends responded only with delight. Every other reaction you could almost predict by zip code—the closer they lived to Manhattan, the brighter the glint in their eye and the deeper the interrogation. Which private school did she attend? Which tutor did you employ to help Sarah write her college essay?

She didn't attend a private school, and I edited her essay—a little bit. I kept that to myself and fended off the inquiries. We did it our way, and we succeeded. For all of my blarney about not suiting up for the rat race, I still used its standards to measure achievement. And then Max died anyway. Max didn't die because of social pressures. Mental illness didn't care where we lived, or which club we joined, or whether Max went to private or public school. For much of the first year after Max died, I remember being mystified by the fact that we had avoided the arms race and gotten destroyed nonetheless.

To be fair to me and Meg, we measured neither Max nor Elizabeth by the academic successes that Sarah achieved. We told all three kids we wanted them to do their best and to find the college that felt right to them. "I don't care where you go," I said many times. "I'm not going to be the one going there." Max felt comfortable at RIT, and that was good enough for his parents. But in all honesty, though I enjoy going to Rochester, though I enjoy being near the lakeshore where Max died, eating the Schaller's fast food and Abbott's frozen custard that sustained him in college, I have to gird myself to set foot on the RIT campus. My memories of Max around the lake are good. My memories of Max at RIT are not.

By my second football season without Max, in 2016, I could tell that I had begun to view his loss from a distance. The art, and it is surely art more than science, of moving forward in life while remaining connected to my dead son is made more difficult because the connection is anchored in my heart. It is a dilemma, a riddle answered only by feel. This is an elevated form of grieving. You must calculate how much of you to leave behind, how much of him to bring with you, how to carry forward while maintaining balance and nimbleness.

I wasn't sure that I liked moving forward. It bothered me when I sensed it around my extended family, in how they didn't bring him up. To this day I try to regularly mention Max around his cousins, hoping to impart to them that he remains a part of us. When I officiated my nephew Evan's wedding in New Mexico in the spring of 2016, I tried to mention Max and got choked up. In the fall, I performed the same duty in New Orleans for my niece Rebecca, my voice faltering only briefly. But when I looked up from my reading, I saw Rebecca squeezing her eyes tightly in an attempt to hold her composure.

Time had created distance between me and Max. I felt it. I no longer gained the same comfort from wearing Max's black-and-white flannel shirt. In the two winters since he died, I had worn it to calm me, to connect me to him. I didn't feel that emotional warmth any longer.

Besides, football season always served as an emotional cocoon that I entered in August and emerged from in December. That mental pod proved to be solitary and resistant to invasion. There's always another story to write, another call to make, another podcast to record. Another plane to catch.

If I wondered whether I had pulled away too quickly, I also had to acknowledge that time moves faster at my age. Days are shorter. Football seasons are shorter. That same fall, our next-door neighbor Jean died at age sixty-nine while traveling abroad with her male companion ("boyfriend" doesn't fit a senior citizen). She had been the ideal neighbor—warm, polite, careful not to encroach on boundaries—and poof! She was gone. Her sensible car sat in her driveway, like a dog waiting for a master who isn't coming home. I began walking out the back door each morning, looking at her car, and saying aloud, "Hi, Jean." And then, "Hi, Max."

After a few weeks, her companion drove into her driveway as Meg and I stood in ours. I hadn't seen him. I walked around the hedge, gave him a hug, and said, "I'm so sorry."

"Yeah, he said, "it's awful. Especially the circumstances."

He looked up at me.

"But YOU know. You have to keep living."

What he said crystallized something that had been in my mind. A day or two before we left for Rebecca's wedding, I went to the cemetery and talked to Max. I teared up and told him I don't know what to do. I have to keep going, but I don't want to leave him behind.

When I first began to notice, it unnerved me. That fall, as everyone in the 312 area code remembers, was the year the Chicago Cubs broke their 108-year-old curse and won the World Series. Meg and I watched with the rest of America. Harry Caray, the Cubs' late play-by-play announcer, remains a presence at Wrigley Field. His caricature is on T-shirts. Fans draw it on posters. At the seventh-inning stretch, as the celebrity of the day leads the fans in the singing of "Take Me Out to the Ball Game," the team shows video of Harry doing the same. It was his tradition. He owned it.

Max may have only tolerated baseball. But he liked Harry Caray. He liked him so much that I bought him a T-shirt when I passed through Chicago. When he and I went there after high school graduation, we ate dinner at Harry Caray's, which is a good steakhouse. We walked there from our hotel.

But as Meg and I watched game 5, the last series game at Wrigley, I couldn't remember why Max liked Harry Caray. That set off a panic in me, that I was losing my memories of him. I was fifty-six years old, and already the information in my brain sometimes sat on a shelf too high for me to reach. I had to go get a chair and stand on it to retrieve whatever nugget I desired. Normally I didn't get upset; doctors always say if you eventually retrieve the information, you're fine. But in this case I panicked. I couldn't text Max and ask him for a reminder.

After several minutes, I remembered: Max liked Harry Caray because Will Ferrell used to impersonate him on *Saturday Night Live*. Max didn't love Will Ferrell, whose talent for breaking through the barrier of discomfort to get a laugh usually left Max feeling discomfited. But he liked him when he did Harry Caray.

That winter we spread the last of Max's ashes. We returned to Steamboat Springs so that Max could make his last visit there. We had been there as a family for more than a dozen winters and a couple of summers, too. Meg and I contacted Josh Berkowitz, the ski instructor who had taught, encouraged, cajoled, teased, and given Max the gift of skiing competence. Even as Max proved his ability to ski the most difficult inclines, his favorite trail remained Why Not, a gentle, winding trail that provides the best views of the Yampa Valley below.

Meg and I followed Josh down Why Not until he pulled off the main drag onto a shortcut through the trees. It was one of the many unmarked shortcuts that Josh had shown Max. Neither Meg nor I had ever noticed it. Josh stamped out M-A-X with his ski boots, and we spread the ashes among the letters. We didn't break down as we had at the cemetery in Fairfield, and we didn't dissolve into comic farce the way we had at Lake Ontario. It just felt right.

I will say this about the cemetery in Fairfield—it had become a wonderful tribute to Max and the love that friends and family had for him. There is a Jewish custom that anyone who visits a gravesite leaves a stone on the grave marker as a record of their visit. As with most Jewish customs, if you ask two scholars for their origin, you will get three answers. In this case, I have two favorites. One is that in the ancient days, rabbis would be considered unclean if they came too close to a corpse. Jews began to mark gravesites with rocks, an early traffic sign, if you will. Another explanation, one that pleases the word geek in me, is that the Hebrew word for "pebble" also means "bond."

Atop Max's headstone and spread all across the base are dozens of smaller stones. After Max's death, Meg began to travel. She took trips to Iceland, to Spain, to Portugal. Shortly before cancer claimed our beloved sister-in-law Annie at the age of fifty-six, she encouraged Meg to take Elizabeth to Paris, where Annie had taken her daughter a few months before. A week after Annie died, they left. When Elizabeth studied abroad in Berlin in her junior year, Meg went there, too.

From every destination she returned with a rock to place at Max's grave. Collecting stones from across the globe became a mission for her. She continues to keep a carved wooden basket in her car filled with rocks from her travels. Among the tokens on Max's grave are rocks from Camelback Mountain in Arizona, the Pacific shore in San Francisco, and Chimney Bluffs State Park, about forty-five minutes east of Rochester. That one is special.

Max took one of his best photos there. The Chimney Bluffs are silt formations that rise above Lake Ontario. They are not permanent—the lake shapes the silt through erosion—and they are not as dramatic in person as they appear in photos. In person they look like structures built in Legoland, scaled-down versions of the real thing. But Max took a photo of the bluffs from a half mile or so that makes them look as majestic as a mountain range. It is a photo that left an impression on us, and I think it may have left one on him. He uploaded it onto the digital photo frame he gave Meg at his last Hanukkah.

His last Hanukkah. That is one serrated phase.

But there is a rock from Chimney Bluffs on Max's grave marker.

Meg remembered a rock for Max as she traveled all over the world. I didn't think to pick up a rock for Max until I got out of my car at the cemetery and walked into the woods that abut the property. As you may have figured out by now, the best expressions of my grief for Max appeared when I sat down at the keyboard. Thoughts began to arrange themselves into prose. That's how my brain works. I began to consider explaining what my grief felt like, to take the reader by the hand, to make grief more understandable. A few days later after the first anniversary of Max's death, I published a piece on Medium. The passage below illustrates the depth of the hole in my innards. No matter how well I processed the loss, he was still gone.

It turns out that understanding death is a poor palliative for grief. The pain of loss patiently waited for me. The pain, no longer camouflaged by the shock and trauma of the event, by the ministrations of friends, by intellectual exercise, had nowhere else to be. I know that Max was sick. He's still gone. The football season that distracted me for six months is over. Max is still not here.

The death of a child upends the life of a family. It is not a tornado, with a path of destruction visible from NewsCopter 7. It is an earthquake, an upheaval that begins in the epicenter of the nuclear family and spreads outward; from the four of us, to Max's three grandparents, to his 14 aunts and uncles and his 19 first cousins, to neighbors who watched him grow up, to teachers and friends within the community, to the friends he made in college and online of whom we learned only after he died.

Earthquakes buckle walls and leave crockery in shards on the floor. We are still trying to repair some of the broken pieces of our lives. Some we have put back together with visible scars. Some we haven't started to fix yet. Some we just swept the debris away. Nothing is as it was.

We are aware of and engaged in the good things that continue to happen to us. Yet the colors of the palette are not quite as vivid, the tones of the instrument not quite as rich. It feels as if we are watching our digital lives on an analog set. There is no antenna to detect the sharper signal. We live our lives with rabbit ears, trying to pull in the daily richness of life through the static.

We nurture the memories we have of Max and live in fear of their finite nature. Time will erode them, as it does all memories. But we have no new ones with which to replace them.

We have learned over the last year that a good number of friends and acquaintances have borne the death of a sibling or parent quietly for years. They have served as confidants, as examples that we can forge ahead, as reassurance that, shattered though we are, we are not alone. We are grateful for the solace they bring, as well as for the many kindnesses, small and large, that have been done for us. Even as the anniversary of Max's death has stirred painful memories, it has provided one small

Photo courtesy of the author

comfort. Only by looking backward can we see that our scars have begun to fade.

That felt pretty raw, and it reads that way. But my philosophy then, as it had been a year earlier, as it is today, is that when it came to grief, I would not worry about bruising the sensibilities of others. Besides, I hadn't set up a website to expound upon my loss again and again. Two more years would pass before I posted another essay on the subject.

One day during my travels during the 2017 football season, I looked at the wallpaper photo on my mobile phone. I had installed it two years earlier, after Max died. We took the photo the day that Sarah graduated from Stanford in June 2014. We are not a photo-taking family. Meg and I bought a video recorder during the kids' early years. We used it haphazardly, and we never look at what we videoed. Which is pretty much like the rest of America, I'd guess.

Max may have loved his Nikon, but he had a natural aversion to photographing people. Besides, once he and Sarah went to college, the number of occasions when the five of us gathered diminished considerably. Often, we took a photo on Thanksgiving Day for the holiday card to go out the next month. But on Thanksgiving Day in 2014, we never got around it. Oh, well. We could use a graduation photo for the holiday card. There'll always be another time to take a family photo.

Until there isn't. Max died three months after Thanksgiving, and in that moment those graduation photos took on a meaning that none of us ever intended. They are the last photos that the five of us took together.

So I set a photo of the three kids as the wallpaper on my phone. Steve Jobs called it wallpaper for a reason. We don't notice it very often. It's a backdrop. It is not typically the focus of your eye. One day, I looked down at my photo, and for the first time in two years, I studied it. What I saw triggered a flow of feeling for Max that sent me to my laptop. I posted the essay on Medium in March 2018.

I Keep Trying to Catch His Eye

Untold times a day I glance at the photo of my son with his sisters, the wallpaper on my phone. His older sister, now employed for four years, a millennial professional with an expense account and a career, stands next to him in cap and gown. She is holding her college diploma, a big smile on her face and the possibilities piling at her feet.

To her left is his younger sister, the high school junior now college junior, the former lifeguard turned history scholar, the camp counselor now preparing for the summer Manhattan internship. She returns the camera's gaze, her grin as radiant as her sister's.

And Max's face remains a mask, staring up and into the distance, away from the camera, the eye he would never meet. Funny—photography was his passion, the most expressive record we have of his life, but only if he were behind the camera.

The girls mature. Our lives evolve. I look at a new haircut and see the gray that had been hiding beneath. My wife, his mother, his rock for 21 years, slowly gets her pins beneath her after absorbing the concussive blow of his death. Max remains in that photo, the earth spinning him away from us with every revolution.

I have visited my son's gravesite in every season. I have taken a selfie of my reflection in the polished black granite of his headstone, tucked in a corner of our temple cemetery. I have stepped delicately through late-winter mud to add one more stone to its ledges. I have seen green blades of grass stuck to it hours after the mower came through. I have seen autumn leaves scattered at its base.

On the raw January Monday that would have been Max's twenty-fourth birthday, what I saw on that marker seared itself on my memory. The dates on the headstone had receded. They no longer felt current. That unnerved me. I had never before visited my son's gravesite nearly three years after he died. I looked at the date 2015 carved into the stone. I thought of how the country had changed paths. Our lives had changed paths. The undertow of time pulls and pulls and takes us away.

I worry that moving on is callous, too black and white, a shrug of acceptance when I should cling to what I can bring with me of my son.

Max would be out of college, presumably, stepping tentatively into adult responsibilities. He never stepped any other way but tentatively. He was accomplished at protecting himself from his fears and demons, until they overwhelmed him at the last.

He tried little that was new. He sat in the same position in the same new chair in our den, cantilevering his pipe-cleaner frame so that his feet rapidly wore a dirt pattern at the edge of the cushion. I worried that Max would struggle after graduation, that he would not be able to gain traction in the adult world. I projected that he would return to us in defeat, unable to find gainful employment.

That attitude, searching for a word somewhere between ignorance and arrogance, is one of the regrets I continue to carry. It is ignorant of how so many college graduates need time to find the right place to start, arrogant in its desire that he meet a standard that he may have been unable to meet.

I am clearheaded that Max died of mental illness, as lethal as cancer and more difficult to fight. I don't believe that my demands of him outweighed my support of him. But what I wouldn't give to have him return to us in defeat. It would beat having him returned to us in Ziploc bags.

Max left out of turn, and the unfairness of his premature death heightened the pain of the loss. We are going forward and Max is not going with us. That is as heartbreaking as it is unavoidable. Our lives go forth without him. We have to live them. To do otherwise, to remain anchored in grief and by grief, would be to lose even more than Max's death already has stripped from us.

If Max's death has taught me anything, it is that life doesn't allow you to remain anchored anywhere. We keep moving, even when all we want to do is remain in a moment, return to a crossroads, undo a regret, say something that would have changed where we stand today.

On the third anniversary of his death, the four of us dined together again. It felt too soon to call it a tradition; the undertow of time will continue to tug at us, separating the four of us as we bob and sway. I am left with my wallpaper. I keep trying to catch his eye. Max continues to look up and away.

The piece went viral, the response to it visceral enough that Medium put a link to it on the front page of the entire site. In journalistic real estate terms, that's Central Park West in Manhattan. Pacific Heights in San Francisco. Knightsbridge in London. Soon Medium asked for an audio version, which, with the guidance of Josh Macri, my podcast producer at ESPN, I was able to provide. I didn't decide to write this book then. But the reaction to that essay gave me the confidence that I could translate typically private, hidden emotions of grief in a way that reached people. That confidence would serve me well in 2018, the following year.

Chapter Nine

The Hilinskis

The epidemic of suicide that has broadsided this generation has meant that there is a greater push against it than has ever been known.

The more we push against it, the faster it comes at us.

We are inundated with advice, memoirs, ways to cope with "every parent's worst nightmare." I never liked that phrase. This is not every parent's worst nightmare. You wake up from a nightmare. I liked better the way that our friend Mary on Cape Cod described it in a note she wrote us soon after Max disappeared. "Losing a child eclipses all of life's tragedies."

Yes.

We sift through the material, saving the items that speak to us, that fit our need for solace, or reassurance, our need for a repository for anger, for guilt, for shame. You want the world to stop spinning. You want the world to stop making memories. The person you love is gone. You get no more. But the world keeps going. You bring of him or her what you can carry. You have no choice but to leave the rest behind.

When news broke in January 2018 that Washington State quarterback Tyler Hilinski had ended his life, I knew my phone would ring. I thought my office would call immediately. No. The call didn't come for a few weeks. But then David Duffey, my editor from the day I walked into the building in 2002, called to discuss the possibility that I write about Hilinski.

Why did I wait for the phone to ring? Why didn't I offer to write the story?

I had no interest in writing the police procedural, the how and where of Tyler's death. It's not because it hit close to home. I had no problems with the vast majority of journalists, print and video, who reported about Max's death. From the beginning, Meg and I agreed that we would hide nothing from anyone. A journalist refusing to comment is, to me anyway, an oxymoron. And sometimes, being on the other side of the transaction made me laugh. When we held the memorial service for Max, nearly a thousand people managed to arrive at our temple at 11 a.m. The reporter from our local paper arrived at 3 p.m. The only quotes in the page 1 story the next day came from our rabbi describing the service.

But I told Duffey no, I wasn't ready to write about Tyler Hilinski. It just didn't feel right.

A couple of months later, *Sports Illustrated* published a story and produced a short documentary about the circumstances surrounding Tyler's death. When I opened the magazine and saw the piece—Greg Bishop wrote it well—I exhaled. Now that *SI* had written the piece, ESPN would have no interest in reprising it. That's how journalism works. We are proprietary that way.

Duff, as we all call my former editor, is patiently persistent. He waited a couple of weeks and called again. This time, he said *College GameDay* had expressed an interest in me doing a piece on Hilinski. That turned my head. *College GameDay* is where college football America congregates to begin its day. I had to listen. When Drew Gallagher, the features producer for the show, called, we batted around a few ideas.

"Look," I said, "you called me to do this story for a reason, because my son killed himself. If you want me because of my knowledge, let me do a story about Tyler's parents. That's who I am an expert about. That's what I know."

Drew, to his credit, understood. Drew, to his credit, assigned me the producer Lauren Stowell, whose talent as a storyteller and in an edit bay is surpassed only by her ability to establish trust and disarm whatever emotional defenses her subjects have erected.

Having agreed to do the story, I delayed contacting Mark Hilinski, Tyler's dad. I didn't feel sheepish about my privacy being violated. It's that I had to work through nearly four decades of trying mightily not to cross the journalistic line, the one drawn to keep the writer out of the story. Plenty of sports columnists in my career would have been out of work if the *I* key on the laptop had been disabled. That wasn't me. Journalistic sensibilities have changed in the internet age. Fewer stories are held at arm's length. Opinions are tolerated, if not encouraged. It took me awhile to get accustomed to a sensibility that goes against a career's worth of training and practice.

All I knew about the Hilinskis is what I read. I knew that, and I knew that grief is personal. I had decided to make my grief public. The Hilinskis seemed to have made that same decision when they cooperated with *SI*. But I didn't know that for sure. The *SI* story focused on their beloved Tyler. The story I wanted to write would be about them, about how they had to learn to put one foot in front of the other again.

Both Drew and I understood that if the Hilinskis had no interest in cooperating, there would be no story. I have written plenty of stories on subjects who didn't want to be interviewed. But I couldn't draw open the curtains on the parental grief of suicide victims if Mark and Kym Hilinski chose to console themselves in private.

However, here I had another unique connection to Mark and Kym Hilinski. My family's grief had been public. So had theirs. The suicides of our children were national news stories. We could relate in a way that other parents, even the parents of other children who ended their lives, could not.

I went over in my head the consolation that Meg and I had received. I thought of what soothed and what didn't. I thought of a number of friends, people we had come to know casually in our two decades in Fairfield, who quietly let us know that they carried with them the sudden, tragic death of a family member: a brother who died many years ago, a child who died in infancy. To have seen them function fully in society without knowing of their loss gave me solace that someday, somehow, we would recover.

I thought of the fathers who had called me, fathers who had lost sons in car accidents and to suicide: Dan Goodgame, now the editor of *Texas Monthly*; Chris Myers of Fox Sports; Mike Lutzenkirchen, whose son Philip had starred on Auburn's national championship team in 2010; Miami Dolphins then–head coach Joe Philbin; my cousin Bryan Maisel; my cousin Dan Einstein in Greenville, South Carolina, thrust onto this road a few years earlier, checked on me regularly. It dawned on me that they had paid it forward, that someone probably had reached out to them, and that my reaching out to the Hilinskis might be the natural order of

things. Maybe I could help them, and maybe writing about helping them might help the readers better understand the dastardly
turn our lives had taken.

I sent an email to Mark Hilinski, telling him a little bit about Max
and explaining that I would like to speak with him about a possible story. He replied to the email with his phone number. I didn't
call immediately. I waited a few days and called on a Sunday night.
We spoke for an hour and ten minutes. Throughout the process of
giving shape to both my story and the video profile, the Hilinskis
couldn't have been more gracious, even as the pieces reflected the
enormous amount of pain they suffered and continue to suffer.

Lauren, the producer, brought a crew, and we spent a day at the
Hilinskis' home in Orange County. And I mean a full day. We got
there in the morning. We began an interview, Mark, Kym, and I
standing around the kitchen counter, just talking. I sat down and
interviewed Mark and Kym individually. Somewhere in there we
broke for lunch, which Mark bought. And late in the afternoon,
we left.

Those interviews were as emotionally intense as any I have conducted in my career. As a print guy who usually works without a
crew, I found having colleagues around me to be not only a luxury
but a great help. I didn't have to worry about a single logistical detail,
details that have tripped me up throughout my career. Let's just say
that, from an early age, I have not been good with gadgetry. When
I was twenty-three years old, I interviewed baseball great Pete Rose
exclusively on consecutive days. The second day, I remembered to
turn on my voice recorder.

In the Hilinskis' home, with a videographer and an audio guy
working for me, with Lauren there to ask the good questions that
had never occurred to me, all I had to do was focus on what Mark

and Kym had to say and how they said it. I listened for what I needed to know from them in order to tell their story and concentrated on delivering what I needed to say in order to help them.

In telling the Hilinskis' story, I realized I could describe to the outside world what this existence feels like. I could take away the binoculars from anyone intimidated by the deaths of Tyler Hilinski and my son Max, and how they died. I could bring them up to the window and have them peer in as the Hilinskis sorted through the wreckage that used to be their life. And by inference, because I am three years further down the road than the Hilinskis, they could peer in at me and see that the pieces of that life can be, as best as possible, reassembled.

It won't be your former life, the good one, the one with healthy children, where mental illness was something that happened in other families. That life is gone. This life, this new life, will never be that full. But it can be fulfilling.

That is what I wanted to convey to the Hilinskis. I thought it might help them, just as it had helped me to talk to parents admitted before me to the Club No One Wants to Join. There was so much I could tell Mark and Kym. There was so much to tell them about this road we are on, this journey we are taking together. Only we don't take it together. We all grieve in our own way. Even as members of a club, we all go separately. The best we can hope for is that we understand each other a little more than others understand us.

There is within that thought the mindset of a journalist. Every journalist filters her story through her own experience, even the ones who strive for pure objectivity.

There is so much I could tell them, and yet I wanted to know how they handled it—for the sake of the story and for my own well-being. Even as I know we all grieve differently, I wanted to peer over their shoulder while we were taking this damnable test to check my answers against theirs.

The column posted approximately a month later.

IRVINE, Calif.—I came of age in the wake of Woodward and Bernstein, when young journalists were taught to be as neutral as the painted highway stripe. After nearly four decades as a sportswriter, I have learned to negotiate a middle ground between my training and my life experience. Some stories demand more of the latter.

I understood that the moment I read last January that Washington State quarterback Tyler Hilinski ended his life. He was a college junior, 21 years old, the second of three children, hundreds of miles away from home.

Almost three years earlier, my son Max ended his life. He was a college junior, the second of three children, 21 years old, hundreds of miles away from home.

Like a winemaker trying to create a structured red, how much of the skin you leave in the juice changes the color and character of the final product. I've got a lot of skin in this one.

There's often an immediate intimacy among parents whose children have ended their lives. We get it. The loss of a child is an awful subject, so awful that it makes people uncomfortable. They don't know what to say. One of the many secrets of The Club No One Wants to Join is that we love to talk about the children we've lost. Talking about them keeps them present.

But people hesitate, sometimes under the guise of protecting the feelings of the bereaved. I would say, always with a smile to smooth the delivery of the sarcasm, "You know, if you hadn't brought Max up, I wouldn't have been thinking of him."

When you live with the awful every moment of every day, the awful becomes everyday. It is no longer so daunting. When someone told me I was living "a parent's worst nightmare," I responded, "No, you wake up from nightmares."

The first time I called Mark Hilinski, Tyler's father, we spoke for 1 hour, 10 minutes. "I had never talked to anybody—in my spot," Mark said later, with a mirthless laugh. "Got emails, got letters, got cards, read a ton. . . . But that was the first time I had talked to anybody that kinda sat over here, and I appreciated it."

Mark's wife, Kym, Tyler's mother, sounded a note of grace. "I'm actually happy that [people] can't understand," she said, "because I would never, ever want anyone to really understand what you and I are going through."

Mark is a bear of a man, personable in the way that most successful salesmen are personable. He is a traditional American Dad. He responds to problems in the stereotypically American Dad way: looking to fix them. Except that this problem, the biggest that he and Kym have ever faced, can't be fixed.

He hates that he can't fix the problem, and he hates that he feels self-pity because he can't fix the problem, and once you go down that rabbit hole it can be a long time before you see sunlight again.

He understands that he is not the first father to lose a son. He understands we live in a world where bad things happen. He and Kym recently attended a memorial for a 20-year-old struck by lightning.

"If you can muster it, that'll put some perspective on you quick," Mark said, "but it doesn't lessen the sadness for me."

Seven months in, that sadness wafts off of Mark and Kym like pollen on a springtime breeze, its residue on every object. I recognized that melancholy. When our son died, his older sister returned to her California home after six weeks. A year later, she confided to us that the house had been so sad she had to leave.

Kym remembers sitting on the plane to go to Pullman after they learned Tyler was gone.

"I didn't mean this against anybody else," Kym said. "I just meant it for me. I said, 'Lord, can you just let the plane crash? Can you just let it crash? I don't want anybody else to die. I'm just fine if I go. I'm fine if I go if I can just be with him.'

"And the plane didn't crash, of course."

For the first month, Kym said, she didn't brush her teeth. She didn't wash her face. Mark wore the same jeans every day. When I heard that, I didn't flinch. The week that Max disappeared, I didn't eat. I lost eight pounds.

As Kym looks back, she understands they are making progress. But one of the first rules of grieving is that everyone grieves differently. Mark feels that all time has done is pile more pain at his door.

Take the spring, when he would get reminders on his phone about Washington State football practice, calendar entries he had made months earlier, before the earthquake that made a debris field of his life. His phone has been a font of sadness. He loved the FaceTime calls from Tyler after practice, or the simple excitement of glancing down and seeing a bigger text bubble from his son.

"That'd mean he had something to say and you were interested in whatever that was," Mark said.

You think about those things when they don't happen.

Mark and Kym Hilinski, as did I, chose to open the door to their grief. I decided to respond to questions because I didn't want anyone to believe I was ashamed of Max. Suicide is an act, not a person. I don't much like the word. It carries more baggage than an Airbus. Our son, and the Hilinskis' son, were so much more than their final acts.

The Hilinskis also speak about their loss in part to publicize the foundation they created in the aftermath of Tyler's death. They already have donations and pledges of more than $100,000 for Hilinski's Hope. The foundation has begun to fund mental health programs for Division I athletes, including at Washington State. Mark and Kym will raise the Cougars flag at Washington State's home opener Saturday, and a Hilinski's Hope flag will hang in Martin Stadium this season.

Mark and Kym go through their phones and computers, looking for pictures of Tyler to post on the foundation website or to provide to news media.

"You go to the hard drive and find the stuff," Mark said. "And then it hits you. There's a finite number of those. You can [post] three a week and you're gonna repeat at some point because there are no new pictures."

They try to stay busy. Kym awakens before dawn and begins to do the work of the foundation, reading and responding to emails, writing thank-you notes for contributions. Mark has dived back into his work, selling software to retailers that curbs employee theft. And they have the football career of their youngest son, Ryan. He is a senior at Orange Lutheran and one of the most sought-after high school quarterbacks in the nation.

On the kitchen counter of the Hilinski home one day last month sat a letter from USC coach Clay Helton, offering Ryan a four-year athletic scholarship. On the tabletop below the TV screen sat a letter from an undergraduate at South Carolina, where Ryan has committed to play, with a healthy donation to Hilinski's Hope. Those are the two poles of the Hilinskis' lives—the loss of Tyler, the rise of Ryan.

"He deserves every bit of the excitement and fun and enjoyment that he's getting," Mark said of Ryan. "That's a good reminder for us to sorta dial it up a little bit."

Maybe the time that has continued to pile pain at Mark's door will turn out to be his friend. As much as you want your life to stop and return to the last time you thought your dead child was safe, the last moment before you got that phone call, it does not. Your life goes on. That continuance includes good moments. The last thing you want to do is acknowledge them or, God forbid, celebrate them. But your emotional muscles respond to happiness without realizing you have no interest in being happy. You catch yourself having a good moment, and then a good hour, and then maybe even a good day.

That might be easy for me to say because I have lived this loss for 3½ years. But I remember. For the first year after Max died, I poured my grief into my laptop. Writers write. I woke early, when the house was quiet and I could hear my thoughts, and I typed—at first nearly every morning, then two or three days a week, tapering until I didn't need to type any more. As I flew out to see the Hilinskis, I returned to my entries seven months after Max died, trying to get a sense of where they were, and read in reverse order chronologically. I read how fragile I was, how slowly I walked, how, on my first reporting trip after returning to work, Oregon head coach Mark Helfrich brought me to tears just by asking me how I was doing. *[More on Helfrich and this trip in the next chapter.]*

Ryan is three games into his senior season, what should be a crowning experience in his young life. But hovering over the family is the role that football might have played in Tyler's death. The Hilinskis had Tyler's brain sent to the Mayo Clinic, which discovered evidence of CTE. It is impossible to know the precise effect of football on the condition of Tyler's brain. But it is easy to make assumptions.

"I remember sitting there just crying, just thinking how did I even say he could ever play football?" Kym said. "Why did I ever even say yes? And, then, I remembered why. . . . They [their sons] fell in love with football. And so that's probably why. I mean, you—when you fall in love with something, you fall in love with something. Right?"

This season, Ryan switched his uniform number to Tyler's No. 3. When he threw his first touchdown pass of the season, his first touchdown pass wearing Tyler's number, Ryan came off the field bawling. Mark went down to the sideline and wrapped his son in a bear hug until Ryan could compose himself.

Orange Lutheran has begun this season 2–1. Ryan plans to graduate in December and enroll at South Carolina in January. Shortly afterward, Mark and Kym will move to Columbia, or maybe Charleston, two hours away. It's an adjustment. Then again, Kym told Ryan that she couldn't bear to set foot in all those Pac-12 stadiums where they had gone to see Tyler.

Wherever Kym is on Mother's Day, she will continue her tradition of skydiving on that day. This year, she and her oldest son, Kelly, went together. They called it Ty-diving. For some people, milestone days can be the hardest. On Easter, Mark, Kym, Kelly and Ryan distributed Tyler's ashes at a lighthouse on Kauai where the five Hilinskis had distributed Kym's mother's ashes several years ago. On Tyler's birthday—May 26—Kym and Kelly climbed Mount Rainier. Tyler had promised Kym they would climb it before he graduated.

He was a son who liked spending time with his mom. In high school, he referred to her as Kymmy Kym. The Tyler that Mark and Kym describe is a sweet boy, the peacekeeper among three brothers, the friend and son who tried to help his brothers, his teammates, anyone in his orbit. When the Washington State coaches compiled a list of the players' cell phone numbers, Tyler gave his mother's number. Every time the team received a text blast about a meeting, or a reminder to show up for training table, or anything else, Kym received it.

"I know you love knowing where I'm gonna be, Mom." Tyler told her. "I know you love getting those texts. And so I'm not gonna put my number down."

These days, Kym spends time with Tyler by walking a mile and a half to the post office. That's when she talks to Tyler. That's when she gets mad at him. She tries to save her tears for the walks. She tries not to cry in front of Ryan any longer. It's hard for any child, even a 17-year-old in a man's body, a leader in the locker room, to watch his parents fall apart.

The other day Mark, Kym and Ryan went to see a movie. Tyler loved movies. On the days he didn't want to be an NFL quarterback or a football coach, he talked about becoming a director. "I was sitting in the middle. Ryan was on my right. Mark was on my left," Kym said. "And we were seeing 'Mission Impossible: Fallout.' You know, shoot, shoot. There's car crashes. Right? But they're fun. And ordering food is fun.

"I remember looking over at Ryan. And he had his hands on his ears like this," she said, raising her hands, elbows jutting forward. "And I thought, 'What is Ryan doing? It's not a shooting scene.'

"And then, I went, oh my gosh, I'm crying. And I'm crying loud. I'm crying because we're at the movies, those things that we loved to do with Tyler that I knew he loved.

"And Ryan was sitting there going, 'My mom was crying. I don't want to listen to my mom cry because I don't know what to do. I don't know how to make it better for her. I can't bring Tyler back. She likes going to the movies. She loves sitting and eating popcorn with me, and Red Vines.'"

She sputtered for a second, and stopped.

"That was not a good day," Kym said.

When the boys were younger, any time they requested to go somewhere—a weekend breakfast, the movies—Kym would say, "Yes, if we ride bikes," or "Yes, if we walk." It was a mom's way of stretching out time with her children. She remembers when Tyler reached the crest of a hill and started coasting down, he would yell, "Downhill freedom!"

He is free now of the demons that plagued him. That's how I think about Max. It has sustained me through many sad moments.

In her fantasy world, Kym is living on a beach with Tyler.

"I don't know how I came up with this phrase. I always say 'coconut and straws,' man, 'coconut and straws,'" Kym said, her eyes glistening, her voice catching. "We would've sold coconuts with straws for the rest of our lives in our swimsuits. And we would've been together. And nothing else would've mattered except he would've been with me, so coconut and straws."

In her fantasy world, Kym Hilinski has kidnapped Ryan and gone to the same beach, or maybe a different one. She has taken his passport from him. He will never play football again.

"And trust me, I've really thought about this," Kym said. "I'm not joking. And I say, 'You can't get back. You're stuck with me.'

"I can't do that. Right? But I have played that scenario out a few times."

I hope those fantasies sound nonsensical to you. That would mean you've never lost a child.

The reaction to my column, and to the profile that ran that weekend on *College GameDay* for more than seven minutes—an unusually long segment on a show where features of two to three minutes are the norm—revealed a lot to me about the nature of grief in general and how we talk, or more accurately don't talk, about suicide.

Within an hour of the column posting, I received a beautiful note—from South Africa. Readers, colleagues, and friends reached out. I know a flood of responses went to the Hilinskis, too. I came to realize that subjecting myself to the Hilinskis' pain, and showing it to the public, generated the reaction from readers and viewers that I had been courageous. I wrote in an earlier chapter that picking up the pieces of your life and continuing on after tragedy is often seen that way. From society's end of the telescope, and that's as close as most people wish to come, continuing to live your life after such a loss is too painful to consider. They believe it is courageous to tell that story.

I understood. That used to be me. But I no longer had the luxury of standing on that side of the telescope. I answered the phone one night in 2015 and discovered that I was thrust into a new existence. That is exactly why it took no courage to tell their story. There is courage in living it, in finding a way to go on in the face of what seems to be, in real time, insurmountable sadness. You summon the strength to do what you must. It is the courage of which we speak when we talk about battling cancer, overcoming poverty, coming to terms with grief, continuing to live with an overwhelming burden.

There isn't much courage in talking about how you get through the day. All of us get through the day. It's just some of us have to work harder to do it. That's the point I am trying to make.

When the Grady School of Journalism at the University of Georgia invited me to speak at a symposium on journalistic courage, I went because they asked, and because I have friends on the faculty, and because I love Athens. But to my mind, journalistic courage is outing a bad guy or holding your ground in front of a public figure who bullies you day after day. In that sense, the only courageous action I took in the entire process occurred when I sent an introductory email to the Hilinskis. I risked getting the figurative door slammed in my face. I didn't know how they would respond. Cold-calling is not easy for me. Forty years into my career, a successful career in which I have built a reputation as a fair journalist, I still have to gin up the nerve to call an interview subject. I don't want to intrude. Well, I *do* want to intrude—that's the nature of journalism. As silly as it may sound, after all these years my stomach churns any time I contact anyone who doesn't know I'm calling and who may not want to be interviewed.

I spoke to a room full of the program's top student journalists, as well as a few faculty. I couldn't have been happier to see my friend Claude Felton, the longtime sports information director at

Georgia, walk in with former football coach and athletic director Vince Dooley, my fellow Mobilian. I tried to explain to everyone that I didn't see this story as courageous in the least.

Living with this grief is what my everyday life is like. My son is gone every day. I am accustomed to his absence. I don't like it. It fits me like wrong-sized shoes. But that absence has become as integral a part of me as our two daughters. I will carry my grief with me throughout the rest of my life.

The Hilinskis continue to pour their grief and their energy into their foundation, Hilinski's Hope, which is raising money to fund mental health programs for collegiate athletes, young men and women who are proving to be especially vulnerable to stress and mental illness. The Hilinskis are finding purpose, living their lives, understanding that good events and bad events will continue to happen. The difference is that they will experience them through the filter of sustained tragedy.

I consider the Hilinskis friends now—another blurring of the journalistic lines—and yet I have continued to write about them. When an injury thrust Ryan into the Gamecocks' starting lineup in the second game of his college career, in September 2019, I traveled to Columbia and wrote about the Hilinskis again. About the instant bond that they established with the rabid South Carolina fan base. That the support the Gamecock fans showed for the Hilinskis has been a rich source of comfort for the family.

Ryan, wearing his brother's number 3 again, raised his right fist and led his team out of the tunnel and onto the field. Kym saw her son at the front of the charge and yelled, "Go big Ty!"

Once she realized what she had yelled, Kym crumpled into her seat and didn't say anything for a long while.

With Ryan running the offense in a 72–10 victory over Charleston Southern, the Gamecocks set a school record by gaining 775 yards of total offense. More important, as a kid six weeks shy of his nineteenth birthday, Ryan showed the emotional maturity he needed to lead a huddle full of older, more experienced teammates.

Mark and Kym's parental needles are very sensitive where Ryan is concerned. They watch him walk into a room and work the people, checking on everyone they see.

"How you doin'? You good?" Ryan would say. Mark remembered Tyler doing the same thing, realizing after his death that it had been a mask, a defense to keep people from seeing him scrabble to gain purchase, trying and failing to find his emotional balance. They see Ryan with a newfound perspective, not getting too high or too low, and hope that means he is stable. Lose one child to suicide, and you're very careful about taking the behavior of your other children at face value. That's just human nature.

South Carolina, and Ryan's career in Columbia, proved to be a good place for the Hilinskis to recuperate. After two seasons, Ryan transferred to Northwestern, strictly a football decision. But even if they hadn't been adopted by the Gamecocks for two years, the Hilinski family still had a great gift that the Maisels do not: a Cougar locker room, a football building full of coaches and support personnel, and a fan base at Washington State, all of whom remember their son as a friend, a teammate, a young man with talent and potential. The Cougars are grief stricken too.

On the last home Saturday of Washington State's 2019 schedule, the program honored the Cougar seniors. It is one of the best of the modern rituals of intercollegiate athletics, no matter the sport. For four (or five) seasons, the parents of the players have bonded with one another in the stands just as the players have bonded in the locker room. Relationships are built.

At the seniors' last home competition, they are introduced to the fans before the game. The senior walks to the middle of the field or court, where family and head coach awaits. Everyone hugs and shakes hands.

On Saturday, November 23, 2019, the Hilinskis returned to Martin Stadium in Pullman to reconnect with the players who continued to compete together after their classmate and friend's death. The Hilinskis reconnected with the parents with whom they had sat in the stands for three seasons. Washington State said goodbye to Tyler Hilinski one final time. If the void left by the death of Tyler felt larger because of his standing as a college quarterback, then the bond of the Washington State players and parents with the Hilinskis, not to mention the love and support of Cougar fans across the nation, might have made that void feel more manageable.

Managing the void is all any of us can do.

Chapter Ten

A Better Person

My career as a sportswriter began in 1981, a long time and many forgettable stories ago. For most of my career, the bigger the moment, the smaller my story got. Certainly, the slower I got. Before my close friend Gene Wojciechowski became a star reporter on ESPN *College GameDay*, he and I covered college football together for more than twenty years. Gene watched me grind in the press box and labeled me "DFL"—dead fuckin' last. There is honor in press-box grinding. Red Smith, the patron saint of my generation of sportswriters, once described our work as easy. "You just open a vein," Smith said, "and bleed." It's a good line, as wry and self-deprecating and clever as Smith himself, a columnist in Philadelphia and New York for about half of the past century.

But when Red Smith got through grinding, he produced copy worthy of Red Smith. When I got through grinding, I felt as if I had written for an English as a second language class. When Texas stunned USC in the 2006 Rose Bowl—basically considered the greatest game of my professional career—I went into utter panic. I sat for two hours before I began a third paragraph. I was forty-five years old, completing my twenty-fifth year as a sportswriter, yet that story took me forever, and years went by before I could bring myself to read it again. It wasn't as bad as I feared. But thinking about it triggered PTSD.

There's also a memory from the next year of being the DFL writer to leave the Fiesta Bowl press box after a national championship game, in which Florida routed Ohio State, 41–14. My dread of big games bothered me. The adrenalin would affect me, cloud my thinking. All I had to do was cover the game. I didn't have to play in it. But in my business, that game is the biggest event of the year. I couldn't handle it. Jealousy of my press box colleagues who seemed to relish these big games nagged at me.

It took me a long time to find a voice—my voice—that I trusted. For years, I interpreted my training to believe my job was not to leave anything out, to tell everything and let the reader decide what was important. What that meant in reality is my stories lacked focus.

My career had extended into its fourth decade before I no longer felt beholden to lay out everything that happened in a game. Only when I decided to emphasize a moment, or a couple of moments, or a theme derived from those moments, did my writing become more compelling. Unconsciously or not, I decided I had acquired the authority to take a stance, to choose those moments.

My game stories became more compelling. I felt as if I had cracked the code. At long last, I felt as if my authority—my "voice"—had sufficient weight to validate my choices.

And then Max died.

Max died and for weeks I set aside my work without any certainty of when I would return. I knew I would return, just not when. Max died in late February, during the college football offseason; the timing allowing me to grieve and remain unfocused. Actually, ESPN allowed me to grieve and remain unfocused. The ESPN ethos allows great latitude to the employee in times of personal crisis, a luxury that I suspect is rare in the American workplace.

When I did return to work, haltingly, in early June, I returned because I felt I was supposed to come back to work. Oregon had lost the national championship game five months earlier. After Marcus Mariota, the Duck quarterback who won the 2014 Heisman, left early for the NFL, Oregon signed a graduate transfer quarterback, Vernon Adams from Eastern Washington, to take over.

I flew out to write the story, even though Oregon, per the orders of head coach Mark Helfrich, didn't want to talk about Adams (he hadn't enrolled yet). Helfrich, with whom I had a good relationship, agreed to an interview even though he had a morning full of meetings that began at 8 a.m. I appeared at his office at 7:30. We spoke for twenty-five minutes; I thanked him and began to close my notebook.

"Can I ask *you* a question?" Helfrich said.

"Sure," I replied.

"How are you doing?" he said.

My throat swelled. My eyes teared, and it was all I could do to croak out an answer. Helfrich had recently lost both of his parents, so his grief remained close to the surface, too. We spoke for another twenty minutes. He was late to his first meeting.

My experience, which I presume is not unique, is that a griever doesn't find closure and then resume his former life. You pick up the shards of your former life, put them on the work table, and see whether you can reassemble something that looks like your life, only with cracks and blemishes. In this case, I tried to reassemble a career, if not the one I had, then something close to it.

I say that because my priorities had changed. The games that had meant so much to me for nearly my adult life, the games that had caused me to eagerly leave my family on nearly every fall weekend for twenty-seven years, the games that I took so seriously that I choked when it came time to write about them, no longer meant as much to me. It felt as if my annual fall shipment of giddy excitement was stuck in a FedEx Ground warehouse somewhere, and I had to make do with the meager supply on hand. Just-in-time emotions, if you will.

I sat in the press box thinking I had seen this game before. I sat there thinking about my grief. I sat there thinking about Max, and about my wife, and about our daughters. I sat there until the game ended, and I went downstairs and, without much emotion and not a lot of interest, picked a topic, wrote a story, uploaded it, closed my laptop, and went back to my hotel.

That sounds robotic, if not grim. My son died. I didn't care as much about my work. My sun no longer rose and set on which team climbed to number one or whether a coach might be fired. Instead of being obsessed with chronicling the authoritative version of the season in weekly installments, I drifted toward stories I found compelling.

And here's the thing: as I cared less, as I held my subjects at arm's length in order to protect my ravaged soul, I found that I could see them better. As my pain became less acute, as my grief had to compete with my decision to propel my life forward, I found my perspective had improved. The historian Jon Meacham, on his 2020 podcast *Hope, Through History*, describes how Winston Churchill led Great Britain through World War II "from this distance, and mountains are usually better viewed from a distance . . . " With distance, I became more clear-eyed in my story choice. I found a tale I wanted to tell, and I told it. It just didn't matter as much to me as it once did.

An aside: when I got into this business, I was the same age as the athletes, and I regarded the coaches as authority figures. As I got older, and my children got older, I saw the coaches as peers. The athletes became contemporaries of my kids, and I treated them as such. I teased them more, tried to make them laugh to get them to relax, just as I would the friends of my children. There is great freedom in that. The college football star is a talented athlete, but he's not mature yet. Today, I approach the story in a lot more straightforward fashion, unencumbered by my subject's stardom.

My newfound empathy for those who suffered like me made me more perceptive of my subjects. When I wasn't covering an event, when I was working on a feature about someone, I began to dive deeper. I began choosing topics from which others might shy, especially as it regarded grief or personal pain. I didn't consciously make the choice. My emotional antennae still may have been in their factory packaging, but my perspective had changed. A couple of months after my interview of Helfrich in Oregon, I returned to the West Coast to write a story about Stanford quarterback Kevin Hogan.

Another aside: I spent the past decade writing a lot about Stanford football. Yes, it is my alma mater. That's one reason I paid close attention to what happened there. The real reason is that I had a daughter enrolled there for eight of the nine seasons from 2010 through 2018. David Shaw, who became head coach there in 2011, did me the great service of having very good teams. The Cardinal won three Pacific-12 Conference Championships in a four-year span. ESPN paid for several trips for me to see Sarah and Elizabeth. The benefits of having my daughters among a relatively small (seven thousand) student body paid dividends here and there. My story about the Hogans is the best example.

Kevin lost his father, Jerry, to cancer in December 2014, the end of his junior season. He had tried to play through his father's illness that fall without confiding in any of his coaches. Hogan didn't play up to the standard he had established in the previous two seasons, when he led the Cardinal to the Pac-12 title and the Rose Bowl. Late in the 2014 season, he left school and flew back to Virginia to say goodbye to his father. When he returned to campus, he played like his old self.

Hogan had a story to tell, but, as an introvert, he didn't have a burning desire to tell it. In normal circumstances, media relations people in university athletic departments try to control every bit of access to student-athletes. And Hogan's story made his gatekeepers especially protective of him, which is their job. Media relations people in my line of work treat the contact info of the players in their charge like nuclear secrets. I explained what I wanted to discuss with Hogan, but I didn't have any confidence that they relayed to him that he could trust how I would handle his story.

A few weeks of back-and-forth, and I began to get frustrated about getting an interview. Hogan knew my daughter Sarah, a year ahead of him at Stanford. I told her one day that I wanted to come out and write about Hogan, but I had no idea whether he understood what I wanted or that I would have a sympathetic ear.

"Oh," she said. "Do you want his number?"

Uh, yeah, that would be nice.

So I got the interview. More important, for the first time in my professional career, I didn't tiptoe around such an emotional topic. When I called to interview his mother, Donna, she broke down as she described her husband's devotion to their son. Within twenty-four hours, she texted me her second thoughts about participating in the story.

"I told you that I had some sense of your loss," I texted her. "We lost our 21-year-son Max six months ago. I have learned that everyone grieves differently. But I didn't hesitate to ask you about Jerry because I now have a sense of what it means to ask, and to answer, and I am not afraid of the emotion in the answers. So I can promise you that I will treat what you said with respect." Here's the lead of the story:

STANFORD, California—Kevin Hogan always made it look easy. As a redshirt freshman quarterback in 2012, he took over a veteran offensive huddle midway through the season and led Stanford to its first Rose Bowl victory in 41 years.

"He's always been pretty quiet," said Minnesota Vikings guard David Yankey, an All-American for the Cardinal that year. "But he just had that kind of natural confidence in his demeanor."

Hogan followed that by leading Stanford to a second consecutive Pac-12 championship in 2013. You could ask a lot of college football fans which quarterback begins this season with the most career FBS victories among active players and not get the right answer. It's not Connor Cook of Michigan State, not Keenan Reynolds of Navy or Cody Kessler of USC or sixth-year man Chuckie Keeton of Utah State or Everett Golson of Notre Dame/Florida State. Once Braxton Miller of Ohio State took his 26 wins to H-back, Hogan moved into first place with 24.

"It just means I'm old," Hogan said. "I've been around a long time."

The calendar isn't always what ages us. It can be what happens along the way.

Stanford struggled for 10 games to find itself last season before winning its final three games. Head coach David Shaw analyzed the difference in Hogan from last year to the captain and on-field coach he has seen this season.

"His shoulders dropped," Shaw said.

A quarterback's shoulders determine the accuracy of his throws. But that's not what Shaw meant. He demonstrated, exhaling loudly and dropping his shoulders. Hogan is not pressing this season. He's no longer trying to match the standard the Cardinal set in his first two seasons. He has gained a perspective for which he paid a dear price.

"You grow up really fast when you know your parent's dying," said Donna Hogan, Kevin's mom.

After ESPN.com published the story, Donna texted me again.

"I'm sitting here in tears," she said. "You were right to tell me to trust you."

Hogan led Stanford to another Pac-12 championship that season. My longtime friend Ed Sherman wrote a piece for the Poynter Institute in which he described me writing about the Hogans while grieving myself. I told Ed, "The key for all of us is to hear the questions before we ask them." I realized that my grief for Max had sharpened my empathy.

That story helped me begin to think about writing publicly about my own experience.

When a piece appears about my grief for Max, or about someone grieving, people say, "That must be so hard to write." No, just the opposite. It is easy to write. The first rule of writing is, "Write what you know." *This is my day.* This is what our life is like. The last place I wanted to inhabit is this post-Max world, but inhabit it we do.

People don't want to acknowledge grief, much less engage with someone immersed in it. If it can happen to someone they know, it could happen to them. Better to make a cursory statement of sorrow and keep moving than to confront the possibility that something this tragic could happen to someone, much less themselves. As I have said throughout this book, by writing about grief, maybe I could demystify it. Once it dawned on me that grief is the love we survivors are left with after our loved one is gone, my outlook on life greatly improved.

Those grief-deniers are the people I began to try to reach. How many? Who knows? But there is no question in my mind that in the years since Max died, I have touched more people than I did in the thirty-four years of my career that preceded his death. Maybe that ability is a gift from Max. Maybe that ability is merely a by-product of his death, an unsentimental way of saying the same thing. It's nicer to think of it as a gift. Regardless of how I choose to explain it, my work has received more praise, and I have received bigger awards, than before Max died.

That statement is a rat's nest of emotions. You don't have to travel very far from that sentence to get to the idea that because of Max's death, I am achieving more professional success. Ask yourself whether you are harvesting your son's death for your benefit, and then count the number of times your stomach flips. I have asked myself that question, more than once. A couple of years after Max died, I spoke at a fundraising reception for the Jordan Porco Foundation, which stages events at colleges and high schools across the nation to teach students how to recognize when their friends are struggling with mental illness. I told the thirty or so people in attendance about Max's death and briefly discussed the scourge of suicide. And I said something, off the cuff, straight from brain to mouth, that astonished me.

"I am a better person now."

I heard myself say it. I recoiled. I paused long enough to regain my equilibrium and stumbled through to the finish. But saying something like that aloud, and thinking how it would sound to Meg, forced me to come to terms with the whole notion of assigning any positive outcome to Max's death.

The ghoulishness of capitalizing on my child's death bothers me less than the cynicism inherent in the premise. Of course, of course, of course, I would prefer to be the same emotionally unwoke troglodyte I was in February 2015 if it meant that Max would still be here. That is a stupidly obvious statement. But that is a false equivalency. I am a skeptic, by nature, striving mightily not to be a cynic. I don't know whether these definitions line up directly with either Merriam or Webster, but in my mind, the difference between a skeptic and a cynic is that a skeptic retains hope, but that hope is wrapped in a protective covering. The skeptic may look and sound and write as if she doesn't care. But it's all pretend, a way to ward off emotional bruises.

A cynic lost hope a long time ago.

I have not lost hope. I am not a cynic. Occasionally I wish I had a cynic's defenses. Any survivor knows that long after you come to terms with the loss, a reminder will come up and slap you upside the head before you even have time to raise your hands in defense.

After you read a story on ESPN.com, a link to that story will sit on the left side of your screen. The link includes the title of the story and when it was posted: 4h for four hours ago, 7d for seven days ago, and so on. I often call up old pieces of mine for research purposes. Since I began working at ESPN in 2002, I have a lot of stories that I may call up. One day in 2018, I needed to check something in a column I wrote about a former Notre Dame linebacker, Manti Te'o, nearly six years earlier. After I clicked out of the story, the link on the left side of the screen had this notation: 2,136d. I looked at that number and I froze. I started adding in my head the number of days that had elapsed since Max died. Once I realized that the number easily cleared a thousand, I was dazed, gobsmacked. He had been dead for more than a thousand days. For those of us of a certain age, that number always has been associated with the Kennedy administration. Max had been dead longer than John F. Kennedy had been president.

Someday I will learn not to read the website so closely.

The truth is, this is my life, and I am writing what I know. The benefits I have found in writing about Max and about grief, and hopefully that the reader has found there, are the reason I have written them. Writers write. This is how I communicate. This is how I process emotion. I type a paragraph and I hit the return key. I look to the bottom left of the screen for the word count. Repeat as necessary.

I am lucky to have the outlet, to know how to utilize my skills to prevent my grief from consuming me. Grief is powerful that way.

It has spawned literature, music, art. You name the art form, and someone has processed his grief through it. I am also lucky that I have endured through my pain and grief to become more emotionally resilient. That comes in handy when you pick up the phone on a November Thursday and discover that your employer has decided to move on.

My nearly two decades at ESPN, which ended in January 2021, filled me with great pride. I loved working there. As a young journalist, I worked at *Sports Illustrated* when it set the national sports agenda. I spent eighteen years—by far the largest chunk of my professional career working at the same place—at ESPN as it set the national sports agenda. When magazine journalism became obsolescent, *SI* didn't know how to pivot. As ESPN confronts the demise of cable television and the transition to streaming, the network is trying to complete a pivot of its own. The pandemic that wreaked havoc on so many businesses in America and around the world took a toll on ESPN, and a bigger toll on Disney, which owns ESPN. My contract expired ten and a half months after the onset of the pandemic. Every contract negotiation depends in part on timing. Mine couldn't have been worse.

Over my last three-year contract, I won two annual writing awards from the Football Writers Association of America, the Associated Press named me one of the ten best columnists in the country, and the Orange Bowl gave me the Edwin Pope Vanguard Media Award. Most important, as regards my tenure at ESPN, I served as the editorial voice of College Football 150, ESPN's multiplatform (television, podcast, website) effort to celebrate the sport's sesquicentennial. College Football 150 resonated with our viewers, readers, and listeners in ways that no one anticipated. I am told that the network made a $12 million profit on the project. So I know the decision couldn't have anything to do with my performance. It would be nice to think that job performance matters when it comes to being evaluated. But ESPN decided to trim or not fill five hundred jobs. The company needed to pare salaries. My contract expired. That's an easy one to pare.

ESPN took great care of me professionally and personally during my tenure. When Max disappeared, the company extended me all the time I needed to recover and every courtesy when I returned. The company will always have my gratitude. The decision to send me down the road hurt my feelings. But that's all it did. As should be clear by now, this is far from the worst thing ever to happen to me. If I'm being honest, I will admit that in the days following the company's decision, I felt flashes of disappointment, humiliation, embarrassment. But if I'm being honest, I never felt longer than a flash of any of those negative emotions. I dealt with my hurt feelings. The rest of knowing how to cope with job loss I credit to Max. In death, my son taught me empathy. He taught me patience. He reordered my priorities.

Chapter Eleven

The Lies We Tell Ourselves

In my unguarded moments, when the mental defenses I have developed through years of practice are taking a nap, the existential fears usually quarantined by common sense and rationality come up for air.

My plane is going to malfunction.

My car will be T-boned at the next intersection.

My romaine lettuce is going to incite an insurrection in my body.

The rational part of my brain understands that air travel is the safest form of mass transit, that the other driver is all but certainly sober and attentive, that a good rinsing will protect me from a Caesar salad gone bad.

But I have one existential fear that resists rational thought, that has built immunity to the actuarial evidence that my loved ones and I will live long, healthy, productive lives.

It is all I can do to keep from screaming in terror that I will lose another child.

"Consuming" does not adequately describe the effect of a child's death. "All-consuming" sounds hollow, too.

I never felt comfortable with the sentiment voiced to me over and over again that our lives would never be the same.

No shit. Our son died. I understand at a gut level, not to mention when I walk past his bedroom several times a day, day after day, that my life has veered jaggedly off course. His room—go up the stairs, take an immediate left—remains his room. It is not a museum. There is no rope across the doorway to protect the contents. We have not removed his clothes from the drawers, his tchotchkes from the top of his chest, his Lego creations from the radiator cover. Lego had a product line for older pre-teens called Bionicles, warriors who lived in a distant solar system. Max built those Bionicles and their vehicles. He read all the Bionicle books, long after he had aged out of the cohort the authors had in mind. As he got older, he began creating his own warrior figures, elaborately styled, colorfully designed men or raptors or some combination thereof. When he left for college, they remained standing guard atop the radiator cover in his room. They stand guard still. I wish they had done a better job of protecting him.

The Bionicles are no more museum pieces than the movie posters and photo collages in his sisters' rooms. We haven't reclaimed their space for our empty nest, either. But whatever wistfulness I feel when I walk into our daughters' rooms is borne of nostalgia, of seeing their girlhoods in split screen with the young women they have become. I walk into Max's room. I toss my pocket change into the Mason jar on his chest. I open and close the windows over his bed, the best kind of New England air conditioning. I don't tarry. I don't stay there in order to connect with him. His room is land that has gone fallow, and yet only now, six years since he walked out of it for the last time, are Meg and I beginning to contemplate making use of the space again.

I don't want it to be a shrine. Our shrines to Max are his photos that hang on the walls of our home, the benches that sit on Lake Ontario and in a neighborhood park, the scholarships that we award annually to high school seniors who attended his elementary school and high school. That is how I feel Max today. To walk into his room is to feel Max yesterday. To walk into his room and connect with him through his belongings or his clothes just isn't how I am wired. Finding the magic in that time machine takes an emotional commitment that I am rarely capable of making. My memories of Max when I walk into his room aren't sepia-toned, gauzily filmed remnants of homage to my former life. They are snapshots ripped out of a family scrapbook, static, aging. My image of the aftermath of Max's death is the one I have described before, of me scuttling about the mental property of my existence, madly scrambling to retain whatever scraps of normality I could from our life's wreckage, trying to maintain some connection to the life we had enjoyed for the twenty-one years he lived.

I am not ready to turn his bedroom into an office, an exercise room, a whatever-you-do-when-your-house-becomes-bigger-than-your-life room. Max's room sits at the top of the stairs, take an immediate left. He's not in it. And I feel as if I have moved on. Moving on is different from moving away. I have moved on. Meg says she will not deal in prepositions, that there is no such thing as getting over, moving on. But I view it as a corollary of the old saying, "Look back, but don't stare." There is the grief that we carry with us, the grief that we will continue to carry until we die. Yet the scar that

Max's death left on me is no longer raw and angry and red. We have just celebrated his sixth birthday without him here. Max in death taught me so much more than he did in life. In life, he taught me patience, as most children do. He taught me that it really made no difference that my only son had next to no interest in sports. He provided me with the occasional video-game tutorial, a ruse he adopted to administer an ass-kicking, his glee barely disguised.

In the years since he died, Max has taught me more, perhaps because class never stops. To say that I have a serenity that I didn't have before might convey the wrong impression. But there's a lot of small stuff that I no longer sweat. I have experienced one of the worst events any human being can endure, and I am still standing. I no longer cede power to situations that used to upset me or make me anxious, be they at work or in the community. I am more open and honest, less afraid of emotions than I was before Max died.

This was never a lesson that I wanted to learn. In childhood, emotion betrayed me, adding the humiliation of tears to whatever perceived injustice caused them to flow in the first place. In adulthood, I kept a lot of emotion at arm's length. You can't do that with grief, the crabgrass of emotion. If you don't deal with grief, it takes over the mental landscape. You deal with grief by honoring it, experiencing it, processing it so that there is room for the rest of your existence.

I have grieved. I continue to grieve, and I feel all the better for it. John Trautwein, a former Red Sox pitcher who lost a son to suicide five years before Max died, now works with high school and college students, helping them to intuit and comprehend signs of mental stress among their peers. He makes a compelling presentation, and I would imagine that his work has saved lives. Trautwein told me he makes the presentation to talk about his son, to keep his son present.

He is lucky. Writing about Max doesn't keep him present for me. I keep thinking that I look back at him at age twenty-one, and he should be closing in on thirty. But writing about Max is how I process grief. And through processing that grief has come a more sanguine life. Perhaps that is the gift that Max gave me and continues to give me every time I type his name. It makes me feel good to think so.

That would be a nice story, all tidied up with a bow, easily digestible for those who stiff-arm the deep emotions of grief. There's just one thing. I don't completely trust this serenity. I know how hard I worked to achieve it. I know the price I paid to gain it. And I know the other lesson that Max taught me in death, a lesson I understood long before the COVID-19 pandemic irreparably altered American society: the folly of believing I have control over what happens to me. As I have regained my equilibrium and learned how to function day to day again, there remains a Post-It note stuck in a corner of my brain, reminding me that I am not living in the world I used to inhabit, the world where bad things don't happen. Once you get wrenched out of that thinking, it's hard to return to it. I am a reasonably rational person, and that helped me greatly to function after Max died. But once you learn that you're one random act from having your world completely upended, it's easy to become unnerved, unglued, and untrusting in what the future holds.

I don't know a lot about Buddhism. In her book *Holy Envy*, Barbara Brown Taylor, an Episcopal priest, explains how teaching a college class on the religions of the world helped her better understand her own faith. I remain especially struck by a tenet of Buddhism, the belief, essentially, that we can't control what happens to us, but we do have the power to control how we respond.

In the wake of the death of my son, I understand how the idea that we have control over our lives is a story we tell ourselves to get through the day. To put a finer point on it, there is so much of our lives that we don't control.

There are so many calamities that could befall us.

We make smart choices.

We exercise appropriate caution.

We floss.

We think that is enough to keep us on life's road without potholes, and we get a call from a sheriff saying our vehicle is sitting in the Charlotte Park lot and Max is nowhere to be found. All those smart choices and all that caution didn't stop all that pain and all those lonely hours.

I believe in my heart of hearts that our two daughters are young, healthy, vibrant, intelligent women who will live long, productive lives. But I don't know that. I can't know that. It is impossible to know. I felt this way before the COVID-19 pandemic made all of us throw a lifetime of societal standards out the window (I think an entire generation will look askance at the handshake). It would be nice to say that Max's death has given me a greater appreciation for the preciousness of life. In fact, I can say that, but I say it without the sugary, greeting-card emotion that usually accompanies that notion. I say it with the realization, hard earned, that there is no law of nature that precludes lightning from striking twice.

In my heart of hearts, right smack next to my unwavering belief in my daughters, is the gnawing certainty of uncertainty. When I play that worst-case scenario out, when I envision that most horrible of what-ifs, I ache more for which one would be my surviving child than I do for me. I have trouble comprehending the loss of two children; I have more trouble imagining how it would feel for my surviving child to have lost two siblings. That's even more difficult for me to imagine as a sixty-one-year-old whose two siblings remain healthy.

It is baked into fatherhood to believe that I can sweep aside the pain that awaits my daughters as they live their lives. I can't. Like most American dads, I always tried to fix the problem. My children are in their twenties, and it took me about that long to figure out the best thing to do is shut up and listen. That makes even more sense when you come to the realization that some problems can't be fixed. They only can be endured. I can understand that the odds are greatly in my favor that they, like I, will awaken tomorrow and continue to live a healthy, vibrant life. But I also understand with piercing clarity that long shots come in. I can't protect my daughters from losing one another to a long shot any more than I could protect my son from the hideous disease that caused him to end his life. All I can do is hope and tell myself a story to get through the day.

There are three ways to approach this realization. One is to live on tenterhooks, fearing every new plane flight, every new car ride, every new head of romaine. So many of us lived that way through the pandemic, and if nothing else, we discovered that the accompanying stress is no way to go through life. One is to live the way most of us do, ignoring the possibility of catastrophe, continuing to bluster through life, depending on blissful ignorance and the lies that we tell ourselves.

I do not want to live with the tension and fear, if not outright terror, that comes with the former. I have learned my lesson in the latter.

That leaves only awareness. That leaves appreciation for what comes, with the understanding that I am guaranteed nothing. It is a precarious perch if one is accustomed to assuming that bad events happen only to others. I have been disabused of that notion. With the pain and education of the last six years, I have learned not to take fortuitous events and good outcomes for granted, even if I genuinely believe I am responsible for their arrival.

It is not my desire to sound as if I have evolved to an elevated plane of bliss and gratitude. The loss that my family and I have experienced feels all too real for that. There's a Buddhist parable that stresses that the sorrow, lamentation, and pain in this world arise from clinging. Those who don't cling are happy. Those who don't cling are without sorrow. Perhaps, as the Buddhists say, attachment is suffering, and I am merely wary of being attached to the notion that I am in control.

Which brings up a story about Max. Quiet by nature and schooled in the arid humor of Bob and Ray, Max sometimes spoke as if he had to pay by the word.

His mom had a bumper sticker that read "Attachment Is Suffering." That sticker sat on the rear of her car for years. And then one day, as Meg and Max approached the car, Meg realized the sticker was gone. She was upset.

"Max, can you believe someone stole that sticker?" she asked.

"Irony," he replied.

Chapter Twelve

Every Day

There are days when my grief is perfectly compartmentalized, German-engineered into place. I understand that we were lucky to have Max for twenty-one years. I understand it and I believe it. Max's death cured me of taking life for granted. I haven't quite reached the ideal to live like you're dyin', as Tim McGraw sang. But I am aware that my life, and the lives of those I love, comes with no warranty.

And there are days when I feel cheated, when the solace that comes from coming to terms with Max's death is a twin blanket on a king bed, when no amount of contortion can keep me comforted.

One December after Max died, Meg and I walked down Sixth Avenue in Manhattan on a frigid Sunday night in the pre-Christmas crush. She wore a faux fur hat she purchased three or four blocks earlier from a guy selling them on the corner. *That's* how cold it was.

As we turned onto Forty-Third Street, Meg recalled the story of how Max as a toddler refused to wear mittens. He came to her, enwrapped fully from the wrists up, and said anxiously, "Fingers cold, Mama! Fingers cold!"

"I remember that," I replied, even as the anecdote slid through the very elaborate security system I have installed to protect my emotions. My stomach churned. I grew quickly and enormously sad. My head went light.

Were the story about one of our two daughters, I would laugh at the memory, at their stubbornness, at the cute verbal construct of a toddler. Were it about someone else's child, I would merely laugh.

But it is about Max, and it is about Max being vulnerable, and it is about nostalgia, and it is about Max when we were young, and none of us knew that, someday, long after he agreed to wear his mittens, long after he went inside and warmed up, long after he grew up, that he would again be in pain, pain that could not be dissipated by a pair of mittens.

Childhood is filled with what might be. The death of a child is filled with what might have been. Same thought, different tense, and yet a crushing change in emotion.

I found a letter on my laptop that I had written to Max in the fall of his freshman year at Warde High School. I wrote it just as classes resumed after the holiday break. Max had been struggling in a couple of courses, at least by his standards. In those days, I was never home during the first week of the year. The college football national championship, which I have covered in its various formats nearly every year since 1987, dragged me away from home a day or two after Christmas for anywhere from four to seven days.

If you have read this far, you have figured out that I consider myself a more facile and intelligent communicator when I type than when I speak. Some of that happened because of circumstance. As our three children grew up, I spent anywhere from seventy-five to ninety nights a year on the road. In this case, I wrote from Fort Lauderdale, where I stayed in a swank waterfront hotel as we awaited the Florida-Oklahoma game that would decide the national championship. As I reread the letter, I think it encapsulates how I felt about him and my general attitude toward parenting.

Dear Max,

I have been thinking about the conversation we had last night. And there are a few things that I want to share with you.

Let me tell you about the Max I know.

The Max I know is funny. He has a well-developed sense of humor. He can quote good comedy from Bob and Ray to Whose Line with some significant stops in between. He gets word play. He gets slapstick. Those are my two favorite forms of comedy, too. Anyone who can make people laugh will go a long way in life. You can make people laugh.

The Max I know is smart. Sure, sometimes you get flustered in exams and make mistakes. That doesn't mean you're not a good student. That means you're human. You're doing well in school, and if you're struggling in any subject, all you have to do is ask for help. I'm not sure we can get you a tutor because every tutor in Fairfield is currently teaching your sister (she has three and is about to get a fourth, for the SAT) but we'll give it a try. The important thing to remember is that you like to read, you're curious and you want to learn. Those traits will take you far in life, too.

The Max I know is kind. You're nice to your sisters. You're nice to Calvin and Cece. You're respectful to me and Mom. Kindness is very important to both of us. The world needs all the kindness it can get its hands on.

The Max I know is sensitive. That's O.K. You come by it natu-rally. Your mom and I are both sensitive people. Sometimes I wish I wasn't. When I was your age, I was embarrassed by it. I used to cry as a teenager, and I couldn't control it, and I couldn't stop, and I just wanted to disappear. I couldn't understand why I dissolved like that. There are times now, as an adult, that I get choked up. Sometimes they are good. Sometimes it's embarrassing. So you are not alone.

The point I am making, Max, is that I believe in you. I am re-ally, really proud that you are my son. You are going to do great things in life. I like the person you are becoming. I like spending time with you.

Mom and I will do everything we can to help you. I understand your trepidation about high school. High school sucks in a lot of ways. There's no getting around it. But you have to go to grow your brain and make your way in life. You don't have to go to Warde. You have to go to the best place we can find for you. If that's Warde, O.K. If not, that's O.K., too.

We will work on it together, the three of us, and figure out the best solution. In the meantime, keep working hard. Keep being the funny, smart, kind, sensitive young man you are. Someday, you will feel comfortable enough to let your guard down. It will happen. Trust us. More important, trust yourself.

Love, Dad

We did look at a couple of private high schools, which essentially called Max's bluff. He also hated change. Faced with the possibility of wiping his board clean and starting anew at a smaller school, he chose to deal with his problems at Warde. He worried and worried and worried about problems, and then he faced them, and then he overcame them. I kept hoping he would learn not only to trust my positive attitude but maybe adopt it. Some of it. A little of it.

I am thankful that my memories of Max are not wrapped in the same optimism that I tried to convey to him. Maybe it's the journalist in me, but I have no interest in remembering just the happy times, in living in the fantasyland of selective memory. If my grief is love, then I love all of the person I grieve, the angst and the wit, the good and the tragic. It takes a strong constitution to live with the truth. A parent's memories of a dead child are like Easter eggs in a video game, with one important distinction: the reward can wobble your knees.

Learning to carry grief comes with a built-in alarm system. You learn that opening this door or tripping that sensor will trigger certain emotions. They may be good ones, of course, although even the good emotions arrive with a tinge of pain, a crust of wistfulness.

But there are some memories that attack without warning, like an American stepping off a British curb, traffic coming from the right when you are looking left. Meg cleaned out a cabinet one day and came across Max's school yearbooks. Our elementary school publishes a softcover yearbook that spotlights the fifth graders, the "graduates," if you will. Alongside a photo of each child there is the child's prediction of where he or she will be in ten years.

They are cute when you read them in the moment, and they are cute when you read them after the ten years have elapsed. Meg handed me the yearbook, and I saw our Max, and even as I read, even as my heart broke again, I did the math.

No. He didn't make it. He didn't live the ten years. He ended his life four months short of the ten years.

There is an odd solace in thinking of all the memories I have from those nine years and eight months, of how he grew from the tall, thin preadolescent in the photo to the six-foot-five man who left us. But it is overwhelmed by the implications of the calendar. A simple exercise in creative writing jumped off the page and punched me in the throat.

By the time of this fifth-grade photo, Max had stopped smiling for the camera. It wasn't merely that he didn't like his picture taken. There was something deeper he didn't like about it, something worse than an affront. When forced by his parents or some other authority figure to sit for a photo, Max displayed the warmth usually reserved for mug shots. In this photo, his eyes are narrowed, his mouth thin, "Get it over with," written across his countenance.

Max wrote that he would be living in San Diego, that he would probably have attended Stanford, and that he would be working in design for Lego or in video games. The utter normalcy of that prediction is soothing. San Diego may sound like a curious choice for a child who grew up six miles from the Long Island Sound. But a half-hour or so north of San Diego sits Legoland, the amusement park that then stood atop his bucket list. We went the summer after sixth grade, when, judging by the sophistication of the attractions and the size of the other children, he had aged out of Legoland's cohort. He couldn't have cared less. He couldn't have been happier to be there.

Max didn't attend Stanford. He did visit it several times, before and during Sarah's years there. He never said anything about being able to gain admission there; he understood that he didn't have the grades. And once he entered college, he moved along from his long-desired goal of designing video games, his generation's equivalent of playing shortstop for the Yankees. College honed and sharpened his desire to take pictures. In one of Max's last classes, he was given an assignment not too far removed from the creative writing in his elementary school yearbook. He was asked to create a self-portrait and write the biographical blurb that would appear on the flap of his book jacket.

He didn't share that assignment with us in life. We found it in his cache of photographic work, in one of the oversized film-paper boxes stacked by his bed. The photo is on the cover of this book jacket. Max is standing on the pier behind his uncle's house, looking out upon Lake Ontario, a mile west of the pier he walked to his death. He is wearing his typical uniform: unbuttoned flannel shirt over a tee, a wide-brimmed walkabout hat perched on his thick mop of hair. That he refused to show his face is just so, so Max.

Max Maisel grew up in the state of Connecticut after his family moved from Dallas, Texas in 1994. Inspired to go into photography by renowned Nature Photographer Don Tudor, he studied at the Rochester Institute of Technology for five years before graduating with a Bachelor's degree in Fine Art Photo.

Five years after he graduated, Max's right leg was badly injured while he was working in Acadia National Park. While this greatly hampered him in his career, he nonetheless continued, becoming a moderately successful photographer in the field of Landscape Photography.

Max is a self-admitted recluse, and has refused most interviews that have been offered to him. This book, Vogel im Kafig, and Surgam Identitem are the only books published by him, and he currently lives alone somewhere in the state of New York.

"Vogel im Kafig" and "Surgam Identitem" are songs from soundtracks of anime that Max loved. The former is German for "Bird in a Cage." The latter is Latin for "I Shall Always Rise." In each is the spirit of someone who has been buffeted by forces and yet refuses to yield. I'd like to think that Max felt that way about himself, that he continued to fight against his struggles and insecurities until he could fight no longer. We just don't know. He didn't tell us much; as yet another example, we knew nothing about his attachment to these sentiments until after he died.

Maybe that's why I think the passage on that imaginary book jacket that better captures him is describing himself as a "moderately successful photographer." It makes his mom and me smile every time we read it. That was Max, every dream dipped in understatement, always convinced the best wouldn't happen. I viewed it as a phase, a defense mechanism against life's vicissitudes. I didn't dare consider it a sign of mental illness. I'm still not sure it was. But my response to his negativity haunts me, sits in my brain as a rebuke of my parenting. All I had for his negativity was positivity. It didn't prove to be enough.

Every year on Max's birthday, January 15, I spend the day thinking about him, about who he might have become. That is a puzzle without a solution. Every birthday is intensely, uniquely sad, but they are all sad, every year. The world's worst subscription.

We treated the first few birthdays as we did the anniversary of the day he died. We turned inward, mostly ignoring phone calls, keeping to ourselves, staying in sweatpants. On what would have been his twenty-sixth birthday, five years after his death, Meg and I decided to go into Manhattan to see a musical. For years, we didn't take advantage of living an hour's drive from the best actors and singers in the theater world. As the kids got older, we tried to take them to see at least one show a year. By the time they were in their upper teens and twenties, we would go to a show during winter vacation.

Max loved the musicals—the spectacle, the clever lyrics, the voices, one more talented than the next.

He had seen his first Broadway musical—*Oklahoma!*—at age eight. We played the soundtrack in the minivan for months before we took the three kids to see the show, embedding the music in their brains. The minute the curtain opened, and Curly began belting, "Oh, What a Beautiful Mornin'," Elizabeth, then five, hopped out of her chair and stood in front of it, mesmerized, for the entire first act.

The next winter, on a frigid February day, the five of us drove past horses standing so still in a snow-covered corral that Sarah wondered aloud, "That horse looks frozen. Is he alive?"

Max, without missing a beat, softly crooned, "Oh, the horses are standing like statues . . ."

Pretty quick for a nine-year-old.

On his last Hanukkah, he gifted me the CD of *A Gentleman's Guide to Love and Murder*, a British amalgam of Agatha Christie, Gilbert and Sullivan, and utter slapstick that he and I had seen together that year and loved. The show so captivated him that he lobbied for *Gentleman's Guide* to be the family Broadway outing that December. He couldn't believe that Meg and I chose another show. Several months after Max died, Meg and I went to see *Gentleman's Guide*. She wanted to see the show that he loved so much.

As the sharp pain of losing Max dulled into a permanent ache, Meg and I found ourselves trying to celebrate Max as much as mourn him. Going to a musical on his birthday seemed like a way to honor him, a way to get out of the house, and a way to signify that our lives had indeed continued. And, since what would have been his twenty-sixth birthday fell on a Wednesday, it seemed like such a good idea that we bought tickets for a matinee as well—one birthday, two musicals.

That morning dawned, the calendar delivering its ominous message, and the last thing I wanted to do was go into New York and watch two musicals. What I wanted to do was put on sweatpants, turn inward, turn off my phone, and have my life turn out differently. But I went—we went—and we had a nice day. The musicals, though well done (duh—it's Broadway), would not have interested Max. But the burgers and milkshakes we had for lunch in his honor would have gotten four stars.

We had that same type of lunch on his birthday the previous year in San Francisco. Lunch becomes ritual becomes tradition.

Max celebrated his twenty-first and final birthday six weeks before he died, "celebrated" being an automatic, yet inaccurate, descriptor. He had begun his slide, the withdrawal from reality that we mistook for independence. During the month of winter break he had barely engaged with me, Meg, or his sisters. I cajoled him into going into Manhattan with me to buy him clothes for a family wedding in May. It would be the last one-on-one time I had with him.

As I said earlier, Max comes from two generations of clothes-horses on his paternal side. I didn't have the closet size or inventory of my father, but I did gain an appreciation of fine clothing from him. Max believed in T-shirts and elastic waistbands, no matter the season. He may have been cutting edge—that pretty much describes athleisure—and one of the last gifts he received came from Lululemon. But Max appreciated the importance of nice clothes enough that he didn't squawk about going into New York.

It was a bitterly cold day, the wind whipping down Madison Avenue from what felt like Canada. There is a cluster of men's clothing stores on Madison just north of Grand Central Station. We darted in and out of them, getting Max fitted for a suit and a couple of pairs of nice slacks. Fitted, because at six-five, 135, Max didn't buy off the rack. There aren't a lot of 40 extra-long suits hanging in men's stores. Max selected a couple of dress shirts and matching ties. We raced across the street against the elements for a pair of Johnston & Murphy loafers.

To this day, when I walk past those stores on Madison, I am hit by a wave of emotion. He never wore any of those clothes. What hadn't been altered, we returned. Now those are some phone calls I won't forget: "Hi, my son bought a pair of shoes a few weeks ago and he died before he wore them. I'd like to return them." You could hear the air go right out of the salesperson.

Max and I declared victory on the clothing front and set out to walk a mile into the teeth of that biting north wind to go to Jackson Hole, a venerable burger joint on the East Side. Yes, we should have taken a cab, but Meg and I like to walk in Manhattan, perhaps because when we lived there we couldn't always afford cabs.

Max and I sat down to eat, our various packages taking up the area around us. As I said, Max and I didn't share a lot of interests, but rarely did I have trouble carrying on a conversation with him. Sometimes I would find myself rushing to fill the silences, but it never felt awkward. I mean, I talk to people for a living. I draw them out. I establish trust. I know how to do it. That day I worked and worked and worked to keep the conversation alive. I felt like a Boy Scout who gathered his logs and twigs and failed to get them lit. My memory is that I lapsed into silence, a little frustrated. We agreed when we left to go straight back to Grand Central. And we went in a cab.

Max turned twenty-one a few days later, a day that, on the outside, he appeared to celebrate, and that, upon our autopsy of his computer, we found to be filled with torment. Drew Barlaam, the oldest child of our closest friends, had been the big brother Max didn't have. Drew, four years older than Max, spent time with him when so few others did. They played a lot of video games together. Drew had a great gift for making Max feel at ease.

On the big day, Drew and a couple of his friends, whom Max knew, took him out for his first legal adult beverage. Let me correct that—his first adult beverage, period. Max had never drunk alcohol. He feared alcohol, for some reason that he never made clear. He certainly grew up around it. The Maisel family in Mobile has been in the wholesale beverage business—beer and energy drinks, mostly—for nearly fifty years. Maisel family gatherings include beer, talk about beer, talk about selling beer, you name it. Not to mention that Max's parents enjoy red wine to a fault.

When Max went out for his birthday, he couldn't make himself take a drink. No one teased him about it. The only one there who refused to forgive Max was Max. Meg found this passage in his computer:

I should be happy. I really should. I got some great gifts for my 21st. I hung out with some friends, the cake was great. And yet . . . well, I'm not. Partly because I lost my nerve before ever trying one alcoholic drink—I got so worked up and anxious thinking about it that I couldn't even bring the glass close. Everyone else was fine with it, and anything but judgmental. But it really put a damper on the night.

Max made unreasonable demands of himself on a daily basis; that he twisted what should have been a seminal moment in his life into a reason for self-flagellation says a lot about him. I admit that I might be deriving too much about my son's personality from that one evening. But it's also just as plausible that his response that night is one more example of how he had begun to slide into his death spiral, of how unreal the world had begun to appear in his eyes. I say all that with the benefit of hindsight, because we also learned after he died of his reluctance to return to school. We know now that a few days after his birthday, his anime auteur died, and Max began to spiral even faster.

I don't anticipate Father's Day with the dread that envelops me in the days leading to Max's birthday, or the day he died. Sarah and Elizabeth perform great work to ensure that Father's Day continues to have its high moments. It surely has its low ones.

My sister-in-law Clare texted me on Father's Day in 2020 to check on me. She wrote that Max had been on her mind as society began to emerge from the cocoon mandated by COVID-19. "I was thinking he would probably love masks," she wrote, "because not only could he hide behind it, he would get a really cool, offbeat, alien/anime one."

I thought about that for a second before I responded.

"He would have gotten a cool mask," I typed. "Well, the Max we knew would have. The great mystery and great sadness is, he would be 26 now and we don't know who he would be."

One of the many ways in which Max's death is the gift that keeps on giving is how the typical discourtesies of aging are magnified. We have crested sixty, Sarah is as old (twenty-nine) as we were when we got married, and Max forever remains stalled. Meg and I were completely cognizant of the day when Elizabeth surpassed Max's lifespan of twenty-one years, thirty-eight days. That became another in a series of milestones on a road we didn't choose to travel.

The burden of losing Max that we collectively and individually carry will bring its weight down upon every major decision that Meg and I make and not a few minor ones. In the first year after Max died, with Sarah working and Elizabeth going to school in the Bay Area, Meg presented taking extended stays in San Francisco not so much as a proposal but as an edict. I would not have argued even if I had disagreed.

Several years on, we continue to spend several weeks a year in San Francisco because that's where the girls are. We are trying to spend time in their orbit, as much as their gravitational pull and emotional tolerance will allow. Our futures, truncated by age, are pegged to theirs. As I wrote in the previous chapter, I count on nothing. But somewhere between the blindness of believing that all will turn out well and the nihilism of refusing to make plans, the actuarial tables suggest that our futures should be pegged to our daughters' lives, the reverse of the way we have lived. That is not a decision unique to us as parents of post-college-age children, and yet Max's death impacts this decision wholly and completely, as his death has impacted everything else since February 2015.

In the fall of 2020, Meg attended a yoga retreat for mothers who lost a child to suicide. During the retreat, she emailed me, Sarah, and Elizabeth.

You should know I am in awe of how the three of you are doing, handling this crushing life blow. I'm not saying "You're fine and done." I know this is a forever thing. We will all continue to deal with this the rest of our lives. But I feel like the four of us have tried to look this squarely in the eye, acknowledging the pain, being patient with each other's grief, giving each other the space as it reverberates in our individual and family lives.

Girls, I give your dad a lot of credit for this. I don't know if a lot of men have worked as hard to develop their EQ [emotional quotient] as your father has. We both knew we couldn't fix this, something most fathers, especially, want/try desperately to do. He has been stating loudly these years to let out the grief, to manage it so it doesn't manage us. He has been open and realistic in facing Max's death and the fallout.

You know only what type of dad you have. I'm here to say, you're lucky. You have a great dad.

This is a lifelong journey, and obviously I am devastated that it's your journey. The path isn't linear. You have zigs, zags, highs, lows. Know that we don't expect you to be "all better," grief box checked, life back on track. All good.

But give yourself credit. You get up every day and face the day. And that's really something.

We love you deeply, unconditionally, through wherever your life takes you. We don't expect you to be anywhere but where you are.

Love you big, Mom

That made me tear up. It made me think that the four of us have handled our own private shitshow as best we can. Each of us, in our own fashion, has gotten comfortable with grief, understood that grief is all we have left of the son and brother we miss so much. I will never be so Pollyannaish as to say that we turned a negative into a positive. That isn't true. As I look back, I think what made the difference for me is that, as the Serenity Prayer suggests, I accepted the thing that I could not change. That became my starting point: Max died. Now what? I tried to suspend my disbelief that this had happened to me, to our family. I treated disbelief as a luxury that I could afford only sparingly.

From there, it's a small distance to seeing grief as love. Max died. I have all this emotion, all this pain, all this sadness. Why do I feel this way? Because I love Max. My grief is my love. That works both ways. It tempered how I handled the painful moments. It made me lean into the low moments, view them as evidence of how I feel about my son to this day. That mindset has helped me process the worst event that has ever happened to me. It carries no guarantees for anyone else. I know full well that what worked for me may stop working at my doorstep. There are no guarantees. There are no guarantees for any of us.

Chapter Thirteen

The Evolution of Coping

When you grieve, you try to make sense of the loss. You search for meaning. You lunge for whatever song, poem, folktale, parable, totem, memory will sustain you as you trudge forward carrying your bag of cement. When you lose someone unexpectedly, be it from a sudden medical condition, an accident, or in my case, an illness the scope of which eluded us, I think you hold that security blanket a little tighter: my loved one is gone, but when I listen to this music, or read that passage, or eat that ice cream, my loved one is still here. The soul of the deceased hovers nearby, where we can reach out for comfort, for reassurance.

The urge to believe that our loved ones remain near us, outside of our mind and memories, as some sort of incorporeal presence, surely goes back as long as people have mourned. We wouldn't continue to use that device if it didn't continue to soothe. And yet I maintain—what's a polite way to say this?—a healthy skepticism.

The journalist/realist in me raises an eyebrow. If it is another lie that we tell ourselves, though, it's not a harmful one. Mourning is hard.

The same goes for the notion of the soul of a loved one inhabiting a living creature. Surely the natural habitat of anthropomorphic animals remains a Disney film. And yet I understand the instinct to take whatever is left of Max in this world and assign it to the rabbit that bounds through the backyard, or a cardinal flying from tree to tree. I have heard both theories.

Meg had a different notion. The dragonfly is the traditional symbol of change, of a transformation that sometimes has been attached to death. Some Native Americans believed dragonflies to be the souls of the dead. After Max died, Meg read a story written to explain death to young children. It told of nymphs swimming in a pond, wondering what happened when their friend suddenly disappeared. Where did they go? Somehow they deduce that the dragonfly flitting above them is their departed friend. The dragonfly can't join them, but he is nearby.

It's a lovely story. Meg found the symbolism appealing, and in that first awful spring and summer, so did I. It became another of my many lures to the golf course. On the course I play, a marshy pond spreads the width and a good chunk of the length of the fifteenth hole, a slight uphill par 3. On most days there's a dragonfly or two flitting about. For a long while, I always kept myself ready to interrupt whatever conversation I engaged in on the walk from tee to green by saying, "Hi, Max!" I was already talking to him on the golf course, anyway.

In that first spring and summer after Max died, when golf served as a coping mechanism for me, I inevitably found myself walking down one fairway after another, quietly talking aloud to him. I would say hello. I would apologize for not comprehending his illness. I would tell him how happy I felt to know he had escaped the pain that had driven him to take such a drastic measure. And, after Meg told me the dragonfly parable, I would look forward to the fifteenth hole. I remember sizing up a twenty-foot birdie putt and seeing a dragonfly dancing about between me and the pin. I settled over the ball and stroked the putt right into the hole. My friend Tom Reilly came over to fist-bump me in that pre-COVID time. I pointed at the dragonfly with a big grin on my face and said, "See? That's Max! He helped me make the putt!"

The smile on Tom's face froze in a rictus hovering somewhere between confusion, sympathy, and concern for my sanity. He got over it. We won the match.

Meg's dear friend Anne gave her a dragonfly necklace, and one day she wore it into the jewelry store of Bob Sussman, our friend who funded the bench in honor of Max in our neighborhood park. Bob called me and offered to make Meg another dragonfly necklace, this one fine jewelry. It may be the piece that means the most to her. It comforts both of us when she wears it. But Meg does have her limits.

The necklace that Bobby made is understated. Elegant. I saw a woman's T-shirt online that had a rendering of a dragonfly with the phrase "Let it be" in script aside it: her symbol, and the title of one of the songs that Meg selected to play at Max's memorial service. I ordered it for Meg. It arrived, and the last way to describe the dragonfly is understated. Meg thanked me, and I never saw the T-shirt again. If I had to muster a guess, I'd say that it is buried so deep in her closet that you would need a team of archaeologists to unearth it.

So we have our dragonflies. Most other forms of memorialization we resisted. The instinct to publicly memorialize a loved one is powerful. Obituary writers understand, even in the immediacy of death, that the family wants the public to know the deceased, to know that she built a business, that as a boy he shook the governor's hand, that she loved gardening, fishing, whatever it is that we think of when we think of the story of a life.

That instinct motivated us, too. We didn't want Max to be defined by the way he died. Well, solely by the way he died. There was so much more to Max than his death spiral. But after our immediate reaction, after the feature writers published their pieces, after the clickchasers posted pieces about the ESPN writer's son, after the news crews packed their gear and drove to the next story, we turned inward. We didn't have it in us to commemorate Max as an inroad to gather public support for a cause. Plenty of people do that, and more power to them. They stage road races, conduct golf tournaments, collect change at convenience stores. Our neighbors, whose son died two years after Max, started holding a cornhole tournament for their friends in their backyard every summer. They made it an afternoon-long event, with beers and food and a big jar to collect donations for their charity. I admired their ability to pivot so quickly, to channel their grief in such a celebratory manner. Putting the tragedy to positive use by raising money or awareness for a cause is effective on several levels. It combats whatever affliction caused the death, and for those so inclined, it helps them process the grief. That's what the Hilinskis began doing almost from the moment they lost their son.

We needed to heal. The only public statement we make comes at the annual Senior Night at our high school, where we announce the winners of the scholarships we fund. Meg makes a short speech describing Max and his illness, and implores the seniors that if they experience depression to seek help, and if they sense their friends are struggling to not be afraid to intervene.

Other than that, for five years, we held no events. It took three years for us to have any semblance of a dinner party. We needed distance, and perspective, and perhaps we needed to prove to ourselves that we could resume a day-to-day existence that our grief didn't dominate. I had no problem writing about my grief, talking about Max, providing a window into what his loss felt like. All that I asked of the audience was a couple of minutes of attention, some empathy. But Meg and I recoiled at the idea of asking people to remember Max by donating money. Fundraising is a learned skill that both of us felt uneasy acquiring. In my brief stints as a nonprofit volunteer, my discomfort with asking for money pushed me to help in ways that fit my skills. I wrote. I spoke in front of a camera or an audience. That's my wheelhouse.

Another thing: the idea of putting our friends and acquaintances on the spot bothered me. I have a long history of not asking for help. That might be my own personal pathology, or it might be ingrained in the American male. You know, the stereotype of men refusing to ask for directions (before Google Maps)? I didn't want to stage a fundraiser because I didn't want to ask for help. Not to mention that asking for something means you have to be prepared to hear a negative response. I don't like rejection, giving it or receiving it. I am better about telling people no than I used to be, and I take hearing it less personally than I used to as well, one more of the skills I have acquired through losing Max. But I don't exactly seek it out, either.

Time passed. Five years. Meg, who has come to love cycling, came up with the idea of an autumn walk / bike ride as a way not only to commemorate Max, not only to raise money, but as a safe way to pinprick the bubbles in which we had secluded ourselves to elude the coronavirus.

A walk or a ride would provide the social distance. We didn't open it to the public. We had neither the desire nor the stomach for the work necessary to obtain town permits or wrangle strangers for a few hours. We liked the intimacy of gathering our friends, people who watched Max grow up, who, as Meg described, placed a hand on our back to steady us in the years after he died.

The weather gods didn't just smile upon us; they wrapped us in a clear, brisk, late-summer New England Saturday. We had everyone meet at one of our town beaches. Fairfield borders the Long Island Sound, a body of water that's prettier to look at than it is to swim in. The temperature hovered in the sixties, accompanied by a wind just chilly enough to let you know it was there. Roughly sixty-five people came, evenly split between walkers and riders. The walkers took a four-and-a-half-mile walk parallel to the beach. The cyclists had the option of a twenty- or forty-mile route, designed by Meg's lifelong friend Brian Collins. The best part may have been that we asked the guys at Super Duper Weenie, Max's favorite fast food, to bring their truck to the beach for our group.

The walkers walked, the cyclists rode, and when we finished, we returned to the beach parking lot, stood around and talked, and stuffed ourselves with hot dogs and fries. Our friends rallied to support us, donating thousands of dollars to two causes that Meg and I selected: the Jordan Porco Foundation, which has created peer counseling programs to stem the national epidemic of suicide among college students; and Operation Hope, which works to fight hunger and housing instability in our area.

Max would have walked; the Max we knew at age twenty-one, anyway. He would have grumbled about it, but he would have walked. Among my last vivid memories of Max is a walk. On Sarah's graduation weekend at Stanford in June 2014, a half-dozen members of our extended family got together to walk the Dish.

I have a photo, taken from behind, of me and Max ascending the trail. We are mottled by shadow. Max is wearing a T-shirt, shorts, and the khaki safari hat that he adored. A small camera bag is slung over his left shoulder. I am on his right, a step ahead of him per usual— walk faster, Max—my posture conveying intent. My memories of that weekend are only good, preserved with care because I know what would happen eight months later. Sarah had family come from across the country to see her graduate. We wined and dined (and wined) all weekend. On Sunday, after the graduation ceremony at Stanford Stadium, after Sarah received her diploma, we took the photos that are the last photos of the five of us. Max would live eight more months.

Max and I stopped going to Nets games about the time that he entered high school. He had more responsibilities, and the allure of ninety-minute (at best) drives in winter weather lessened as the Nets began to sink to the bottom of the NBA standings for what would be a decade or so of—what's the polite word?—*uninspiring* basketball. (They stank.) On Father's Day in 2008, Meg asked each of the kids to write me a note about . . . me, what they appreciated about me being their dad. Max wrote me four single-spaced paragraphs. To give you an idea of how carefully Max guarded his thoughts, he scrawled on the back of the envelope, "For dad's eyes ONLY." Inside, at the top of the note, in 24-point boldface, he wrote, "MOM DO NOT READ THIS. I'M NOT KIDDING."

The boy knew his mother.

Dad,

I'm never good at these sorts of things. It's not in my nature to be sappy at this age. Maybe it comes later, when I'm an adult. But since I know it will make you happy, I'll do the best I can, so here goes:

Nearly seven years ago—in other words, just under half of my life ago, I barely got to have what would be called "quality time" with you. Oh, there were those board game nights we had, but for a while, it seemed that you and I barely had time to ourselves together. That's why I'm glad those Nets games came around. It's during those car rides to and from, and during the game itself, that I think I got to know "you" you, not "parent or worker" you. We bonded over Jack Benny, Bob & Ray, and Suspense (all old radio shows we listened to on Sirius) during those trips, and I found a side of you that I barely knew existed. And this was further amplified during the trips to San Diego and D.C. Being in your company for those trips furthered the experience of the vacations, and I think it is times like these that I cannot find fault with you at all; the atmosphere of those times makes it impossible. I only regret that we cannot have that atmosphere more.

And I know all too well that that atmosphere can't always exist (I'd be naïve to think it could). I feel bad about it. I feel bad during the fallings out we sometimes have because I know you're thinking in the long run, and sometimes I can't see that far ahead. I wish I could, though. Life would be much better that way.

So I guess I'll wrap it up here with a few simple words: Thank You. For everything.

Your son,
Max

I read this letter when Max wrote it. Loved it. I am sure I read it again. And I moved on. I threw it in the file labeled "MAX" in the family file cabinet, where it languished in the dark, forgotten, pretty much like the Nets. I didn't think about the note again until Meg found it as I wrote this book.

Max, Mom didn't read it until 2020. Promise.

And now, of course, I am bowled over by the love in it. I am so, so glad that we have it. And I am so, so disappointed and angry with myself that I didn't make a way to spend more time with Max when he made it clear that he wanted to do that. Reading the letter now reminds me that my nostalgia for Max's childhood is tinged—no, not tinged, soaked—in equal measures of warmth and sadness, love and regret, and wondering what was so damn important that I didn't make his wish a priority. I don't ask myself, "What was I thinking?" It's clear I wasn't thinking. I wasn't prioritizing. I was chasing my career tail, holing myself in my attic office, churning out copy to feed the insatiable maw of the website.

That reminds me of a story from Max's childhood. It's October 2000. I finagled an assignment to cover number-two Virginia Tech, with its Heisman favorite quarterback, Michael Vick, playing at Syracuse. Max, a first grader, came with me to spend the weekend with his maternal grandparents. We left early enough on the five-hour drive to give me a cushion to deliver Max to his Oma and Opa's house just off the Syracuse campus before I drove over to interview Virginia Tech head coach Frank Beamer at the team hotel.

Except that we ran into highway construction en route. It became clear to me that I couldn't drop Max off without being late for the interview. I decided to take Max with me to the interview. So we had The Talk, as much as you can have The Talk with a first grader. I went over with him what he would need to do.

"OK, Max. We are going to meet Coach Beamer in the hotel. When I introduce you, you have to look him in the eye and shake his hand. Got it?"

"Yeah."

"Can't give him the dead fish handshake, Max. It's got to be firm. You understand?"

He nodded in the rearview mirror. We practiced, me reaching back from the driver's seat while driving.

"Once I start interviewing him, I need you to sit quietly and be patient."

"OK."

We pulled into the hotel right on time. Beamer came into the lobby, walked over, realized that the little kid next to me belonged to me, raised his eyebrow ever so slightly, and off we marched to the hotel ballroom, already set for the team dinner, to do the interview.

We sat down at a round dining table. Beamer sat on my left, Max on my right. I looked at Max, reminded him what we talked about in the car, and he understood. He would not say a word. And he didn't. As Beamer began to answer my first question, Max hopped out of his chair—and climbed into my lap. I wrapped my right arm around his torso, continued taking my left-handed notes, and looked over at Beamer. He gave just the slightest smirk. And that's how I interviewed the coach of the number-two-ranked Virginia Tech Hokies for the next fifteen minutes.

Hey, Max held up his end of the deal. He never said a word.

As the years went on, I am sure I immersed myself in doing dad stuff, like making a living. I loved my work. I catered to my ambition at the expense of my marriage and family, like most American men of my generation. That was the role model I had. I remember feeling the same way about not seeing my father, at about the same age Max was when he wrote me. As a father of grown children, I fully understand the choices my father made. It's not that I forgive him—my adolescent yearning for him never reached the level of blame, so I hesitate to use the concept of forgiveness. Besides, I am cognizant that, in my twenties, when Dad asked me to travel with him on a couple of business trips, I said no. I had a job, and my ambitions took precedent over my desire to join him. We know where that apple fell.

The difference, of course, is that my relationship with my father played out over nearly half a century. We adapted as our roles evolved. And no matter how our careers got in the way, how the normal miscommunications and misinterpretations of human relations may have waylaid our intentions, we completed the full arc of our time together. My dad lived to be eighty-one.

Max didn't have an arc. The timeline of his life hadn't come close to its apogee.

As with any life cut short, the survivors are left with no way to undo what has been done, to ameliorate failures, to apologize, to recognize with age that the course of our journey needs correction. Experience may be an excellent teacher, but in this case it's a harsh one. I don't interpret my son understatedly wishing for more time with me as a harbinger of his fate. I just read a loving note from a fourteen-year-old boy who wishes he had more time with his dad, and I can't even call him and take him to lunch.

Our digital society bemoans the loss of letters and notes as we text and tweet our way through life. But it's not all bad. Last year, I amended my Twitter profile to add a mention that I had begun writing this book. Out of the blue, Max's online friends began to contact me. Joe DeVader, who lives in the Kansas City area, said they never referred to him as Max until after he died. During their chats, Max was "Exo," because his screen name was ExoRaikou, Raikou being Max's favorite Pokémon.

Joe described Max on their Youmacon trips, how, because of his height and his signature safari-style hat, "They were the first time most of us really realized just how TALL Max was," Joe said, "how he towered over every single one of us, it wasn't even a contest. We used to joke about how if we ever got separated in a crowd all we had to do was look up and find his hat to regroup."

Each year, the group remembers Max on his birthday and on the anniversary of his death. In 2017, sixteen of them assembled in the Kansas City area for a week to hang out.

"This was the first time many of us had gathered together since Max's passing," Joe said, "and so we decided to spend one of the nights huddled around the table one by one talking about Max. A sort of memorial service of our own, if you will. Even that, two whole years later, had most of us in tears by the end. A lot of things were said, a lot of emotions were put out into the open. At the end we went outside and Matt poured a bottle of beer onto the ground, even though" (as he put it), "Max'd probably think this was a kind of dumb thing to do."

The online group remains together, closer than ever. They think of Max when they play his favorite video games. "Whenever a player character in a Fire Emblem game is allowed a custom name," Anneke Weweler said, "I name them Max, as a small way of sharing the game with him." Anneke, who lives in western Canada, created another, more permanent tribute to Max. She got a tattoo of Raikou just above her ankle.

"For me, tattoos are a way to carry stories and art throughout my life," Anneke wrote.

"His story is one of many I choose to carry with me."

I don't grope for words very often, as you can tell, but I struggle to explain why those emails mean so much to me. As I sit at my desk and type this passage, warmth and joy spread through my body. It may be that for nearly six years, we had so few people outside of our family who could commiserate with us. Hearing from Joe and Anneke made real the notion that Max did have friends. Max had friends who cared for him, loved him, and remember him. It would have been nice to know that when he lived. It would have been really nice to go meet with them when they gathered in Kansas City. It's wonderful to know that he remains a part of their lives.

I received an email from a college student in Florida named Al, who said Max had grown into a close friend over the internet. Max ended his life when Al was fourteen, and their age difference doesn't concern me. As I said earlier, Max remained socially immature. To this day, Al wrote in an email, Max "remains one of my closest and best-est friends I've ever had (saying that as someone who didn't have many friends as a child due to social disabilities). It was so much easier to be friends with someone you couldn't see, and that loved to just settle for talking about your favorite shows or games. I feel like that was something both Max and I could relate to."

She certainly had Max pegged.

There is a flip side to hearing from Max's friends. As much as their emails soothed me, they also are a reminder that we watch Max's friends and contemporaries mature into adults, spouses, parents, while Max remains fixed in amber as a twenty-one-year-old. That delivers its own brand of heartache. Al told me that Max knew her as Alex. Alex grew up and matured into Al. Alex doesn't really exist anymore. Time has passed, and we don't get to see Max make that same transition.

I have tried not to make this a maudlin story. I'm not a big fan of maudlin. My whole approach to my grief has been the opposite. You can't do maudlin without sadness, and there's enough sadness in Max's death to soak a thousand handkerchiefs. But as I began to view my grief as an expression of love, my sadness diminished. Often when I think of Max these days, I get wistful. The collaboration of Steve Martin and Harry Bliss on a book of cartoons, *A Wealth of Pigeons*, published in 2020, made me yearn for Max. Martin's unparalleled ability to blend the cerebral and the goofy in a medium that Max loved would have been irresistible for him. Though Bill Watterson stopped drawing *Calvin and Hobbes* shortly before Max's second birthday, Max devoured those strips. He read and reread our paperback copy of *The Authoritative Calvin and Hobbes*, and I'm reasonably sure that Max would have ranked the three-volume, hardback, slipcovered set of the ten years of comic strips to be among his favorite Bar Mitzvah gifts.

In most ways, however, time has allowed us to gain the perspective we needed. In so many ways, 2020, the year of the pandemic, the year of a nastily dyspeptic election that seemed to only highlight the gulfs that have formed in American society, the year I suffered a detached retina, the year ESPN told me it wanted a divorce after nearly two decades, that year couldn't end soon enough. And yet, much as I began this story, when we went to my nephew's wedding only two weeks after that poor fisherman came across Max's body, we have to celebrate the good things that happened in that godforsaken year as well. The changes that the pandemic wrought on society writ large will last long after the vaccines allow us to return to our regular day-to-day existence. The changes that the pandemic wrought on our family accelerated the methodical pace of healing that we had accepted over time.

Both girls may have been professionals with their own lives in San Francisco, but first Elizabeth, then Sarah fled the West Coast in the spring of 2020 and came back to our home in Connecticut. That delighted Meg and me as parents who suddenly received the gift of time with their adult children. Sarah and Elizabeth didn't exactly share our delight. Trading independence for safety means you're in your twenties and living with your parents. They have their own lives and as adults, can make their own decisions. That's how each decided to bring someone new to the family.

Five years had passed since Cece died, only months after Max. Meg had begun to fully engage her wanderlust, one very effective way she soothed her pain. Somehow the topic of dogs arose.

"We're not getting another dog," Meg said.

"We who?" I said. "If I want a dog, I'm getting a dog."

"If *you* want a dog," she replied, "*you* are going to take care of it. I am done."

It was the same argument we had had twenty-five years earlier about where to live. I travel for work, so I depend on her to handle our day-to-day life within our home. Meg has the travel bug, as I said, and she didn't want to be tied down by a dog or cat (or if you think about it, husband). I comforted myself with the knowledge that, once I stopped working, I would look into getting a puppy.

A puppy is an experience that we never gave our kids. We adopted Cece when she was five years old. The kids reminded us regularly, in the way that kids air their grievances long after their childhood had concluded, that we had never had a puppy. When the pandemic struck, and their social lives screeched to a halt, both girls decided, as did much of America, to get a puppy.

Elizabeth is an impulse shopper. She never wavered as to what kind of dog she wanted. She has been in love with corgis since she wore braces. In June, Elizabeth brought home Bubba. I think the name is a salute to her southern heritage. Sarah had been harboring the same idea. In August, she brought home a cavapoo (half Cavalier King Charles spaniel, half poodle) named Archie. There's a story there.

On the day that Sarah brought Archie home, I had a Zoom meeting for the Honors Court, the committee that selects inductees into the College Football Hall of Fame. The president of the National Football Foundation, which operates the hall, is legendary NFL quarterback Archie Manning. There is no more gracious person on this earth than Archie Manning. That evening, he sent me a text thanking me for participating in the meeting. I received it as all of us sat on the patio watching the eight-week-old puppy cavort. I took a picture of Sarah holding Archie and sent it to Manning: "Meet my daughter Sarah's puppy picked up today—Archie!"

"I'm honored!" he replied.

Bubba and Archie injected equal amounts of energy and love into the lives of all four of us. Bubba, coming from a breed of herding dogs, appoints himself in charge of every room he enters. He is smart, attentive, stubborn, and absolutely in love with Elizabeth. Archie, in all likelihood the runt of his litter (at five months he finally surpassed six pounds, a long way from the more typical fifteen-to-twenty-pound range of his breed), made up in love what he lacked in size. He can't wait to meet every single person he sees, his tail whipping like a windshield wiper on 11, his excitement translating into a wave of good feeling that wafts over everyone. He is the perfect antidote for sadness.

Both puppies have given light and love to their owners and helped propel our girls into their future and out of their grief. It is everything a parent would hope. What I couldn't have predicted is that the puppies did the same for me and Meg. She laughed more in the first few months after the puppies came into our home than she had in the previous five years. And not hesitant, polite laughter, either. I'm talking unrestrained glee, the sort set loose by the love, the surprises, the slapstick physical comedy that puppies provide.

Were the puppies mischievous? Of course. Testing the limits? Of course. Peeing on the rugs, the wooden floors, the bathroom floors, and, while in our arms, occasionally on our shirts? Of course. Whether it's an early glance at grandparenting or the freedom that Max has taught us in not sweating the small stuff, I don't know, but we didn't care. We just cleaned it up and looked at the girls like, "How's training going?"

When you put it that way, it sounds more like grandparenting. So does the part where Meg enjoys them greatly, loves them fiercely, and yet isn't the main caregiver. Win-win.

Just as I have tried not to make this a maudlin story, I didn't intend to conclude the book with a manufactured happy ending. We are far from living happily ever after. We will always live somewhat in shadow. But if we are to allow that good things will continue to happen to us, then we are not going to cheat ourselves. My timing in writing a book about Max coincided with the arrival of Bubba and Archie in our lives. Max would have adored them, even if he would have shown it by referring to them as "stupid mutts," same as he did with Cece.

Love arrives in many forms: child to parent, sibling to sibling, spouse to spouse, parent to child, pet to owner, and back again. We are enriched by them all. When the worst happens, and all you are left with is memories and yearning, it soothes me to realize why I hurt so badly. I love Max. I always will. My grief is the most tangible evidence I have of that love.

Acknowledgments

For several years, people asked if I would write a book about Max. I dissembled, sidestepped, and otherwise failed to answer. I needed perspective. I needed to heal. I needed to heal sufficiently enough to write about Max without feeling as if the book itself served as the method of healing. I didn't want to write as an act of catharsis. And then, in January 2020, Meg and I went to lunch in suburban Chicago with Sue Shattock, one of my dearest college friends. Sue didn't so much urge me to write about Max as demand it. Thanks, Shoe.

Gene Wojciechowski and Mark Schlabach, my ESPN college football colleagues, prolific authors, and great friends, provided me with support and guidance. Mark introduced me to Nena Madonia, the agent whose enthusiasm and sharp eye put me on the path to this book. Nena read my first proposal and insisted that I stop writing as if I were reporting on someone else. "I want to know about you and Max," she said. She was right. When Nena left Dupree Miller last year, she left me in the legendarily capable hands of Jan Miller. I thank Jan and Ali Kominsky for their work and wisdom. Thanks to Elena Nachmanoff for her unending support and her unending network of media contacts. Elena led me to Nicole Dewey, who has served me well as publicist, consigliere, and hand-holder.

Dan Ambrosio at Hachette believed in this book from the get-go. Surely the publishing industry has an award for an editor who can work his magic during a pandemic with young children at home while moving residences. Thanks as well to Amber Morris for holding my hand through the book's production and to Carrie Watterson for her copy edits. I'd like to think I fought the *Chicago Manual of Style* to a draw.

Thanks to Lauren Reynolds and Joy Russo at ESPN.com, for looking the other way as I wrote the book. My former editors, current sounding boards, and forever Texan friends David Duffey and Dave Wilson endured my occasional abruptness and attempts at sardonic humor with their characteristic patience and good cheer. My lifelong friend Kevin Sack of the *New York Times* provided emotional support and writing wisdom even as he researched a book of his own.

At home in Fairfield, Brian and Linda Barlaam, Tom and Ellen Reilly, and Karen and Kenny Ferleger have been there for the Maisels for many years. Their support after Max died and as I began to write has been more than meaningful. Adam Simon and Ab Igram served as dependable cheerleaders and great sources of confidence.

My greatest fear is that the extended Maisel and Murray families would leave Max where he left us. In fact, they continue to honor his memory and lift the four of us up, especially at those family events where his absence is tangible. Their love has infused the four of us time and again.

Ah, the four of us. Sarah and Elizabeth have made room for my writing this book even as it intruded on their private grieving. I also owe them for their service as shrewd editors and founts of memory where mine failed. I am so very proud of them. Meg gave me the emotional permission to write this book. Her patience to read through this book's several iterations, even as each one sharpened the pain of Max's loss, may be the most remarkable example of the many sacrifices she has made for me. She also served as a deep well of memories. She remains my biggest cheerleader, and I hope I am hers. Marrying her proved I am smarter than I look.